GOOD CITIZENS

Also by Thich Nhat Hanh in Aleph

Nothing to Do, Nowhere to Go: Waking Up to Who You Are

The Blooming of a Lotus: Essential Guided Meditations for Mindfulness, Healing, and Transformation

The World We Have

Fidelity: How to Create a Loving Relationship That Lasts

Answers from the Heart

How to Fight

No Mud, No Lotus: The Art of Transforming Suffering

Work: How to Find Joy and Meaning in Each Hour of the Day

GOOD CITIZENS

CREATING ENLIGHTENED SOCIETY

THICH NHAT HANH

ALEPH

ALEPH

ALEPH BOOK COMPANY
An independent publishing firm
promoted by ***Rupa Publications India***

First published by Parallax Press in 2012.

Published in India in 2023
by Aleph Book Company
7/16 Ansari Road, Daryaganj
New Delhi 110 002

ISBN: 978-93-95853-93-4

1 3 5 7 9 10 8 6 4 2

For sale in India only.

Printed in India.

CONTENTS

FOREWORD

Many years ago, after burning out from political activism, in my search for a spiritual teacher who could guide me on how to 'be peace' rather than 'fight for peace', I arrived at a retreat for artists at the Ojai Foundation in California. In the five days that Thich Nhat Hanh taught there, I felt for the first time that rather than merely having a concept or notion of peace, I truly *experienced* peace. Each day we walked in meditative awareness among the sage bushes in the foothills of the Los Padres mountain, ate meals in silence, contemplated existential questions, and learnt how to live happily in the present moment.

Thay (as he is known to his students—it is pronounced like the first half of 'Thailand') taught by his example, his metaphors. and his practical, poetic, philosophical words. He taught us to cultivate the energy of mindfulness which would allow us, even in the most mundane of activities, to touch the miracle of life in the present moment.

When I returned home, I wrote him a letter to say that if he was interested in visiting India I would be happy to arrange something for him. As it happened, he had been planning to make a pilgrimage, 'In the Footsteps of the Buddha', and he requested me to organize this journey. It was in those thirty-five days of travel in close proximity that I came to see that I had found my spiritual guide, someone who blended everyday activities with a spiritual significance, someone who epitomized 'Engaged Buddhism'. His insights allowed me to link my inner practice to my outer social, political, and ecological concerns. As I discovered, I was not the only one whom he had affected in this way.

Thay had been instrumental in influencing Martin Luther King Jr. to come out against the war in Vietnam (which is Thay's homeland); in fact, King nominated him for the Nobel Peace prize in 1967, a year when it was not conferred on anyone. His Holiness the Dalai Lama said about Thay that 'he shows us the connection between a person's inner peace and peace on earth'. He has been revolutionary, being one of the first monks in Vietnam to ride a bicycle, to change the language of liturgy from classical Chinese to Vietnamese, to bring much greater gender equity in the Buddhist sangha (community), and even to introduce practices such as hugging meditation in order to make the Dharma more accessible to Americans. Unique in many ways, Thich Nhat Hanh was once described by another Zen master, Richard Baker Roshi, as a cross between a cloud, a snail, and a piece of heavy machinery.

On the actual path of the Buddha, Thay allowed me to understand the Buddha as a human being: one who had struggled with the existential questions of his time and discovered a path of awakening. Thay suggested that I continue this practice of pilgrimage that the Buddha had suggested; it would help me understand the Buddha and his teachings better. Each winter since 1988, I have gone on pilgrimage along the path of the Buddha, and at some time during each year I have gone on retreat with Thich Nhat Hanh.

As I got to know the Buddha better, he struck me as having been a practical man, whose core teachings were ways to overcome suffering and attain happiness, peace, and liberation. His concerns were rooted in our human experience, and not in metaphysical speculations on the existence of God or questions about eternity.

His discovery of the non-self and the interdependent nature of reality—for which Thich Nhat Hanh coined the word 'interbeing'—and his teaching that this understanding can be gained by one's own effort through the practices of mindfulness, concentration, and insight were revolutionary at the time. They continue to be counter-intuitive in a world where so much emphasis is placed on individuality and the self.

Thich Nhat Hanh has taken the ancient teachings of the Buddha, developed in India 2,600 years ago, and made them relevant to our time. The perennial questions of what binds us to suffering and what can give us a sense of inner freedom and awakening remain; but the means of practice have been skilfully adapted. Thich Nhat Hanh has taken many of the practices out of the monastaries and secularized them for an everyday audience. His school of Zen Buddhism, rooted in the 'Mind Only' (Vijñānavāda) School of Mahayana Buddhism, speaks about 'Store Consciousness' which holds many seeds, both wholesome and unwholesome. The basis of Thay's practice is to water the seeds of mindfulness, thereby becoming aware of our mental formations as they arise. In this way we become aware of the roots of those mental states and, in an internal weeding of our mind's garden, we cull or transform the unwholesome seeds and cultivate or quicken the wholesome ones.

Thay has made the Buddha Dharma accessible to people from all walks of life, among them teachers, psychotherapists, lawyers, businessmen and -women, prisoners, parents, and children. This has helped build a worldwide community of practitioners, both lay and monastic. In India, besides having regular gatherings of practitioners, we hold retreats and 'Days of Mindfulness', especially in the field of education and applied ethics.

Thay's simple yet articulate exposition and explanation of complex concepts makes him an artist with words. His poetry speaks eloquently to our hearts and minds. His deceptively simple teachings help make such simple acts as smiling and conscious breathing into practices of self-calming and of deep seeing.

Shantum Seth
New Delhi

1

WHY WE NEED A GLOBAL ETHIC

MINDFULNESS, CONCENTRATION, AND INSIGHT

The world in which we live is globalized. Economies halfway around the world affect our own. Our politics, education, and cultural consumption happen on a global scale. Our ethics and morality also need to be globalized. A new global order calls for a new global ethic. A global ethic is the key to addressing the true difficulties of our time.

Around the world, we are facing climate change, terrorism, and wars between people of different religions. Fanaticism, discrimination, division, violence, economic crises, and the destruction of the environment affect us all. We have to look deeply into these sufferings so we can make good decisions and conduct ourselves wisely. We have to sit down together, as people of many traditions, to find the causes of global suffering. If we look deeply with clarity, calm, and peace, we can see the causes of our suffering, uproot and transform them, and find a way out.

A GLOBAL OFFERING

We are many different cultures and nations, each with its own values, ways of behaving, and criteria for ethical conduct. Every country and every culture can offer something beautiful. It will take all of our collective wisdom to make a global code of ethics. With insight from all the world's people and traditions, we can create a global ethic that is based on mutual respect.

Some people base their ethics on their religion. If you believe there is a deity that decides what is right and wrong regardless of what you observe, then you only need to follow the rules laid out by that religion to engage in right action. Others follow a scientific or utilitarian approach, looking only at what is a logical consequence of their actions. A Buddhist contribution to global ethics is different from both of these. It is based on observing and understanding the world with mindfulness, concentration, and insight. It begins with an awareness of the nonduality of subject and object, and the interconnectedness of all things. It is a practice that can be accepted by everyone, regardless of whether or not you believe in a god. When you train yourself in this practice, you will see that you have more freedom.

APPLYING BUDDHIST ETHICS IN DAILY LIFE

We created the term "Engaged Buddhism during the Vietnam War. As monks, nuns, and laypeople during the war, many of us practiced sitting and walking meditation. But we would hear the bombs falling around us, and the cries of the children and adults who were wounded. To meditate is to be aware of what is going on. What was going on around us was the suffering of many people and the destruction of life. So we were motivated by the desire to do something to relieve the suffering within us and around us. We wanted to serve others and we wanted to practice sitting and walking meditation to give us the stability and peace we needed to go out of the temple and help relieve this suffering. We walked mindfully right alongside suffering, in the places where people were still running under the bombs. We practiced mindful breathing as we cared for children wounded by guns or bombs. If we hadn't practiced while we served, we would have lost ourselves, become burnt out and we would not have been able to help anyone.

Engaged Buddhism was born from this difficult situation; we wanted to maintain our practice while responding to the suffering around us. Engaged Buddhism isn't just Buddhism that's involved in social problems. But engaged Buddhism means we practice mindfulness wherever we are, whatever we are doing, at any time. When we are alone, walking, sitting, drinking our tea, or making our breakfast, that can also be engaged Buddhism. We practice this way not only for ourselves but also to preserve ourselves so that we are able to help others and be connected with all life. Engaged Buddhism is not just self-help. It helps us feel stronger and more stable and also more connected to others and committed to the happiness of all beings.

Engaged Buddhism is Buddhism that penetrates into life. If Buddhism is not engaged, it's not real Buddhism. This is the attitude of the *bodhisattvas,* beings whose whole intention and actions are to relieve suffering. We practice meditation and mindfulness not only for ourselves; we practice to relieve the suffering of all beings and of the Earth itself. With the insight of interbeing—that we are inherently interconnected with all other beings—we know that when other people suffer less, we suffer less. And when we suffer less, other people suffer less.

Now, as well as Engaged Buddhism, we are using the term "Applied Buddhism." "Applied" is a word that is often used in science, and we deliberately use it here as a way of saying that our understanding of reality can be used to help clarify and find a way to transform every situation. In Buddhism, there is something that can be used in every circumstance to shed light on the situation and help solve the problem. There is a way to handle every situation with compassion and understanding so that suffering can be lessened. That is the essence of Applied Buddhism.

THE STARTING POINT FOR A BUDDHIST ETHIC

Mindfulness is the basis of a Buddhist Ethic. What does being mindful mean? It means, first of all, that we stop and observe deeply what is happening in the present moment. If we do this, we can see the suffering that is inside us and around us. We can practice looking deeply with concentration in order to see the causes of this suffering. We need to understand suffering in order to know what kind of action we can take to relieve it. We can use the insight of others, the mindfulness of our Sangha—our larger community of practitioners—to share our insight and understand what kind of action can lead to the transformation of that suffering. When we have collective insight, it will help us see the mutually beneficial path that will lead to the cessation of suffering, not only for one person, but for all of us.

THE VIRTUOUS PATH

In Vietnamese, we translate ethics as *dao due,* the virtuous path. *Due* means virtue in the sense of honesty, integrity, and understanding. The word is small but it implies a lot—forgiveness, compassion, tolerance, and a sense of common humanity—all the good things that everyone needs. The path should be able to provide the kind of virtuous conduct that will help us to transform and to bring a happy life to everyone. When we have the characteristics of someone who is virtuous, we don't make people suffer. This kind of virtue offers us a. guideline, a way of behaving that doesn't cause suffering to others or to ourselves.

Another way to translate ethics is *luong li,* which means the behavior of humans to each other. *Luong* means the morality of humans and *li* means the basic principles that lead to correct behavior and correct action. When you put the two phrases together, you get *dao li luong thuong,* which means moral behavior that everyone agrees to. *Thuong* means common, ordinary, something everybody can accept, about which there's a consensus. Ethics are something consistent; they don't change from day to day. So this means a kind of permanent ethics, basic principles we can agree upon that lead to more understanding and acceptance.

MINDFULNESS, CONCENTRATION, AND INSIGHT

From the time of his first teaching delivered to his first disciples, the Buddha was very clear arid practical about how we can transform our difficulties, both individually and collectively. He focused on how we put the teachings into practice in our everyday lives. That is ethics. Practice is key because practice generates mindfulness, concentration, and insight. These three energies are the foundation of all Buddhist practice and Buddhist Ethics. We cannot speak about Buddhist Ethics without speaking of these three energies. Mindfulness, concentration, and insight help us build a path that will lead to peace and happiness, transformation and healing. It is so important that we don't focus on ethics in the abstract. Our basic practice is the practice of generating the energy of mindfulness, concentration, and insight. We rely on our insight to guide us and help us bring compassion, understanding, harmony, and peace to ourselves and to the world.

Recently, a Christian theologian asked me how to bring about a global spirituality. The person who interviewed me seemed to distinguish between the spiritual and the ethical, but there is always a relationship between the two. Anything can be spiritual. When I pick up my tea in mindfulness, when I look at my tea mindfully, and begin to drink my tea in mindfulness, tea drinking becomes very spiritual. When I brush my teeth in mindfulness, aware that it's wonderful to have the time to enjoy brushing my teeth, aware that I'm alive, aware that the wonders of life are all around me, and aware that I can brush with love and joy, then tooth-brushing becomes spiritual. When you go to the toilet, defecating or urinating, if you are mindful, this can also be very spiritual. So there's a deep link between the ethical and the spiritual. If you can't see the spiritual in the ethical, your ethics may be empty. You may live by this ethical code but you don't know why, and so you can't enjoy it. If your ethical and spiritual practices are connected, you will be able to follow your ethical path and be nourished by it.

THE BUDDHA'S FIRST TEACHING

Hundreds of years ago, under a sacred fig tree in Bodh Gaya, India, the Buddha woke up; he realized deep awakening. His first thought upon awakening was the realization that every living being has this capacity to wake up. He wanted to create a path that would help others realize insight and enlightenment. The Buddha did not want to create a religion. To follow a path you don't have to believe in a creator.

Alter the Buddha was enlightened, he enjoyed sitting under the Bodhi tree, doing walking meditation along the banks of the Neranjara River, and visiting a nearby lotus pond. The children from nearby Uruvela village would come to visit him. He sat and ate fruit with them and gave them teachings in the form of stories. He wanted to share his experience of practice and awakening with his closest five friends and old partners in practice. He heard they were now living in the Deer Park near Benares. It took him about two weeks to walk from Bodh Gaya to the Deer Park. I imagine that he enjoyed every step.

In his very first teaching to his five friends, the Buddha talked about the path of ethics. He said that the path to insight and enlightenment was the Noble Eightfold Path, also called the Eight Ways of Correct Practice. The Eightfold Path is the fourth of the Buddha's Four Noble Truths. If we understand the Four Noble Truths and use their insight to inform our actions in our daily lives, then we are on the path to peace and happiness.

2

THE FOUR NOBLE TRUTHS

A PATH TO ACTION

The Buddha's very first teaching was about the Four Noble Truths. These truths are the foundation of Buddhism's contribution to a global ethic. The Four Noble Truths are: ill-being exists; there are causes of ill-being; ill-being can be overcome; there is a path to the cessation of ill-being.

The Four Noble Truths, including the Noble Eightfold Path contained in the Fourth Noble Truth, are the Buddha's strategy for handling and relieving suffering. The truths are called "noble," *arya* in Sanskrit, because they lead to the end of suffering. The Four Noble Truths are about suffering, but they are also about happiness. Suffering exists, and we can *do* something to relieve the suffering within us and around us. Happiness, transformation, and healing are possible. These truths encourage us to act in order to create the happiness we want. They offer an ethical path to our own transformation.

HAPPINESS AND SUFFERING INTER-ARE

If happiness is possible, why does the Buddha talk first about suffering and ill-being? Why doesn't he just speak about happiness and the path leading to happiness? The Buddha starts with suffering because he knew that happiness and suffering are linked to each other. They inter-are. Suffering contains happiness. Happiness contains suffering. Suffering can be useful. It can teach us the compassion and understanding that are necessary for insight and happiness.

NONDUALITY

Happiness and suffering are not opposites. This kind of nondualistic thinking is one of the key elements of a Buddhist contribution to a global ethic. The good is not possible without the bad. Good exists because bad exists. The Buddha taught that good and bad are products of our minds, not objective realities. There are many pairs of opposites like this, such as being and nonbeing. We tend to think that being is the opposite of nonbeing. We can't have the notion of being unless we have the notion of nonbeing. We can't have the notion of left without the notion of right. But in fact, reality transcends both being and nonbeing. Being and nonbeing are simply notions; they are two sides of the same reality.

Consider the left and the right. You cannot eliminate the right and keep only the left. Imagine you have a pencil and you are determined to eliminate the right side of the pencil by cutting it in half. As soon as you have thrown one half away, the cut end of the piece that remains becomes the new right. Wherever there is left, there is right. The same is true with good and evil. The notion of goodness and the notion of evil are born from each other. Reality transcends the notions of good and evil.

Subject and object are another pair of opposites. We tend to think of our consciousness as something inside us and the world as something outside. We assume that subject and object exist independently of each other. But subject and object are not separate. They give rise to each other. Reality transcends both. If we observe reality over time and truly taste the teaching of nonduality, we have right understanding. Once we have this view, the first aspect of the Noble Eightfold Path, then the other aspects of the Path easily follow. Right Thinking, Right Speech, Right Action, Right livelihood, Right Diligence, Right Mindfulness, and Right (Concentration all arise when we have Right View. The Buddhist contribution to a global ethic contains no dogmas. It doesn't say that it is right and everything else is wrong. This understanding is what the Buddha discovered from deep practice and deep observation. We each need to practice mindfulness and deep observation so that we can know the truth for ourselves and not just follow someone else's teaching.

EACH TRUTH CONTAINS THE OTHERS

The nondual nature of reality is also part of the Four Noble Truths. Although there are four truths, each truth contains the others; they can't be considered completely separately hum each other. If you fully understand one Noble Truth, you understand all four. If you really begin to understand suffering, you are already beginning to understand the path to its cessation. The four truths inter-are. Each one contains the others.

The First Noble Truth is ill-being. The Second Noble Truth is the causes of ill-being, the thoughts and actions that put us on the path leading to ill-being. The Third Noble Truth is well -being, the cessation of ill-being. The Fourth Noble Truth is the path leading to well-being, the Noble Eightfold Path.

The Second Noble Truth is the action that leads to suffering, and the Fourth Noble Truth is the action that leads to well-being, so in a sense they are two pairs of cause and effect. The Second Noble Truth (the path of ill-being) leads us to the First (ill-being), and the Fourth Noble Truth (the Noble Eightfold Path), leads us to the Third (well-being, the cessation of ill-being). Either we are walking the Noble Path or we are on the ignoble path that brings suffering to ourselves and others. We are always on one path or the other.

MINDFUL BREATHING: THE FOUR NOBLE TRUTHS AS A PATH TO ACTION

The Four Noble Truths can't simply be understood intellectually. They contain key ideas, such as nonduality, emptiness, no-self, interbeing, and signlessness, that can only be understood through practice. The foundational practice of the Buddha is mindful breathing. Before we can commit to or practice any ethical action, we need to begin with our breath. Awareness of our breath is the first practical ethical action available to us. This is the only way we can begin to truly understand the basic suffering of human beings and how we might transform it.

When we look at all the suffering around us, at poverty, violence, or climate change, we may want to solve these things immediately. We want to *do* something. But to do something effectively and ethically, we need to be our best selves in order to be able to handle the suffering.

Being able to stop, to breathe, and to walk or move in mindfulness are the keys to the practice. They can be done anywhere, at any time. We can say:

Breathing in, I know this is my in-breath.
Breathing out, I know this is my out-breath.

It's very simple, but very effective. When we bring our attention to our in-breath and our out-breath, we stop thinking of the past; we stop thinking of the future; and we begin to come home to ourselves. Coming home to ourselves is the first thing we need to do, even for politicians, scientists, or economists. Don't think this practice doesn't apply to you. If we don't go home to ourselves, we can't be at our best and serve the world in the best way. We have to *be* ourselves to be our best. Our quality of being is the foundation for the quality of our actions.

Breathing in, I'm aware of my whole body.
Breathing out, I'm aware of my whole body.

Breathing mindfully brings us back to our bodies. We have to acknowledge our bodies first because tension and suffering accumulate in the body. Breathing in this way, we create a kind of family reunion between mind and body. The mind becomes an embodied mind.

If we are truly aware, we know there is tension and pain in our bodies. We can't do our best if we don't know how to release the tension and the pain in ourselves.

Breathing in, I'm aware of tension in my body.
Breathing out, I release all the tension in my body.

We can do something right away to improve ourselves and release our tension and suffering so we can see and act more clearly. With our mindful breathing, body and mind come together, established in the here and now, and we can more easily handle the difficult situations in our lives. Mindful breathing brings more well-being into our bodies. In one breath we can recognize and release the tension within us.

We can use our in-breath and out-breath to help us notice the painful feelings inside us. With our in-breath we can acknowledge these feelings and with our out-breath we can let them go.

Breathing in, I am aware of a painful feeling arising.
Breathing out, I release the painful feeling.

This is a nonviolent and gentle way to help our bodies release tension and pain.

It is possible to practice mindful breathing in order to produce a feeling of joy, a feeling of happiness. When we are well-nourished and know how to create joy, then we are strong enough to handle the deep pain within ourselves and the world.

With one in-breath and out-breath, we can practice all the Four Noble Truths: we acknowledge our tension or pain and call it by its true name; we release it and let well-being arise.

3

THE FIRST NOBLE TRUTH

THE ROLE OF SUFFERING

The First Noble Truth is the truth of ill-being; there is suffering in this world. Ill-being is translated from the Sanskrit word *dukkha.* How did the Buddha discover this truth? When he looked around him he saw poverty disease, old age, and death. We all see these things in the course of our lives. Suffering is a reality. If we don't accept this truth, we can't progress further. There is suffering inside us and around us.

Instead of trying to escape into metaphysical questions such as, "Who created the world?" and "What is the purpose of life?" the Buddha began with the truth he saw around him. This is the first ethical guideline: *we have to observe deeply what is happening around us before we can understand its causes and hope to transform it.*

Instead of sending our minds far away, we can notice what we can see in the present moment and we can call it by its true name. This is a concrete action, not a theoretical philosophy. We can look deeply and see where there is suffering. If we can be truly aware of the suffering and call it by its true name, it is very helpful. Then we will know exactly what kind of medicine, what kind of healing we need in order to deal with our suffering and bring about *sukha,* well-being. Revealing the truth about dukkha will bring about the truth of the cessation of dukkha.

ALL IS NOT SUFFERING

There are those who say that everything is suffering. This is not true. It's an exaggeration of what the Buddha said. The Buddha said that there is suffering, but he didn't say that's all there is. There are causes that bring suffering about, and it's possible to arrive at the state of the absence of these causes. Of course we shouldn't dream that one day we'll have one hundred percent happiness and not a single drop of suffering. There is always something. But we can handle suffering and happiness in an artful way.

WE CAN'T REMOVE ALL THE SUFFERING

It's a mistake to think that we can only be happy if we remove all the suffering. There are a number of things we're unhappy about, but there are also a lot of things that bring us joy. So waking up this morning, sitting quietly and peacefully with a friend—that is happiness. But it doesn't mean that everybody is totally empty of suffering. Each of us has some amount of suffering, but we handle it with beauty. Suffering is present now, but happiness is also present now. If we say that life is only suffering, it's not correct. But if we say that life is only happiness, it's also not correct. There are both, and they each play their role. If we never knew what hunger was, we could never enjoy having something to eat. We can eat properly and happily when we're really hungry. But if we feel that we already have enough in our stomachs, we won't feel so happy when we eat. We can't wait to be happy until we remove one hundred percent of suffering. That moment will never exist.

SIDDHARTHA'S STORY

There are many stories of Prince Siddhartha, the man who became the Buddha. A lot of these stories begin by saying Siddhartha was a protected prince who went for a walk one day outside the palace and saw illness, old age, and death for the first time. The realization of these sufferings led him to such sadness and despair that he wanted to become a monk to help people find a way out of suffering. That version of the story is too naive for me. Siddhartha was a bright and intelligent young man. It can't be true that he never saw anyone who was sick and it's unlikely that in his twenty-nine years he had never seen anyone die.

His father was a king. But a king doesn't really have so much power as we might think. There might be government ministers who are corrupt and prevent difficulties from being resolved. So even if you're the king, you can't resolve all the sufferings of your people. There are so many people who are poor or who are hungry. Many situations are complicated. Siddhartha could see that even if you're the king, you can't resolve all the difficulties and bring happiness to everyone. So he made a determination to find a real path that *could* bring happiness to everyone. That is the reason he searched for a way. For me this is closer to reality than saying that a twenty-nine-year-old man, very intelligent and bright, good at martial arts, well-versed in literature, and many other things, would never have seen anyone sick or dying.

WHAT IS SUFFERING?

Buddhist teachers have traditionally described suffering as birth, old age, sickness, death, being separated from those we love, and having to be with those we hate. All of these things can cause suffering, but they are not the only sources of suffering. Despair is a form of suffering; worry is a form of suffering; and depression is a form of suffering. Often, without even being aware of it, you build up a number of difficulties in your body and your mind. Stress, tension, and fear can accumulate in our bodies and minds and cause us to suffer.

Violence is also a form of suffering. Violence is an energy that wants to destroy, to punish the other person because the other person dared to make you suffer. That irritation in you truly exists. The desire to destroy or to punish is there in everyone. It exists in our society and in each of us. Terrorism is this desire in the extreme. At the basis of terrorism there is wrong perception, violence, anxiety, and restlessness. All of these feelings exist together in one person. If you have been watering these seeds of violence and anxiety, it only takes a small amount of wrong perception about another person or group and you're ready to blow yourself up and kill other people.

Just before the invasion of Iraq in 2003, I gave a lecture at an interreligious peace gathering in France. I said, "You are normal adults and children living in this city. Imagine you know that in perhaps twenty-four hours bombs could be dropping on you and your city could be under attack. You know there are warships blockading your coastline. You would be living in constant fear." Even though there's no bombardment yet, those who are living in these cities already feel terrified. Before a single bomb has dropped, the one or two million people in the city already feel the threat of bombardment. That is a kind of terrorism. No one who goes to war is innocent of creating terror.

Violence and anger exist in each of us and they radiate outward. If we have more of the energy of violence, we suffer more. If we have less, we suffer less. The violence, stress, and anxiety in us don't just cause suffering for ourselves, but also for our loved ones and those around us. Our anger and violence can ripple out and even cause suffering to strangers. We have many sufferings and it is important to call them by their true names so that we can acknowledge our suffering and see its real causes.

THE GLOBAL SUFFERINGS OF OUR TIME

There are many examples of global suffering. The destruction of the environment for generations to come is a disease of our time. Terrorism is also a sickness of our time. There are violence and anger within us, and anger can manifest as terrorism. An act of terrorism is an act of violence, but it is also an act of despair. Religious war is also a form of global suffering. Fanaticism, discrimination, division, violence, and economic crises are all causing global suffering. Hunger, ill-health, and poverty around the world are causing so much suffering. The destruction of human life and the ecosystem, and the many social injustices, all cause great suffering on a global scale.

Suppose we ask a politician to talk to us about the situation in terms of the First Noble Truth. She or he might mention unemployment, crime, or a health crisis. When we speak about ill-being, however, we want to go deeper. The politician might only be talking about the symptoms of suffering, not the roots.

Ethical Buddhism goes deeper. It is very personal and very

specific. We want to talk about the many ways we can make ethical choices in each moment. This is why we begin with personal suffering and how it manifests as tension and pain in the body and mind. This is something right in front of us at this very moment.

We need to abolish poverty and social injustice, and to deal with the problems of global warming and economic recession. But we need to begin with the painful feelings we carry inside us. We have to deal with these things first. If they're not dealt with, we may inadvertently cause more suffering when we're trying to relieve it. The Buddha didn't begin his first teaching with the suffering of social injustice, poverty, and hunger, although he cared very much about these things. He began with the lack of peace within our own bodies and minds. We want to deal with suffering realistically and at the roots.

OUR SUFFERINGS ARE CONNECTED

We want to call each suffering by its true name. Our sufferings do not exist separately; each is interlinked and interdependent with the others. For instance, the violence in an unhappy family can be linked to the stress of each person. Each parent is too stressed; they have no peace, no calm. Just one word that irritates the other can begin an escalation. So the suffering and the quarreling in a family don't begin with unkindness, they begin with one person's pain and stress. That stress is then watered by the stress of the other family members, and irritation and violence grow. So there is an interconnection, an interdependence of things. The suffering of one family is not only inside the family, but it's linked with many other things.

WHAT IS SUFFERING MADE OF?

People always ask, "Why should we call suffering noble? Is there anything noble in suffering?" The answer is that when we look into it deeply, we see that suffering is made only of non-suffering elements. The Buddha did not say that everything is suffering. That would not be accurate. He only said that there *is* suffering in us. The implication of this truth isn't that we should give up and die. Rather, the Buddha wanted us to acknowledge and share our difficulties. All of us suffer deeply and many of us walk around with a constant sense of ill-being.

Dukkha is often spoken of in terms of birth and death, old-age, sickness, and so on. But birth and death are part of life. And because we accept life we have to accept birth and death. So they're not exactly ill-being. Whether or not something makes us suffer often depends on how we look at it. Our suffering is made up of non-suffering elements.

SUFFERING IS MADE OF NON-SUFFERING ELEMENTS

There is great joy in us, even in those things that contain suffering. For example, the Buddha saw that old age contained suffering. But I'm old and I'm so happy. I have found that old age is something very delicious. When we get old, we don't have all the excitement and stress that young people may have. We have more maturity and we have learned from years of unskillful experience to be more skillful. So old age is wonderful. When you are a young person, you are like a young creek, and you meet many rocks, many obstacles and difficulties on your way. You hurry to get past these obstacles and get to the ocean. But as the creek moves down through the fields, it becomes larger and calmer and it can enjoy the reflection of the sky. It's wonderful. You will arrive at the sea anyway so enjoy the journey. Enjoy the sunshine, the sunset, the moon, the birds, the trees, and the many beauties along the way. Taste every moment of your daily life. Old age can be very enjoyable.

We also say that illness is suffering. But disease may strengthen your immune system, helping you cope with later infections. When a person is ill a lot as a child, sometimes they become a very strong teenager. Also, being ill is often the only way we take time to rest. When you are sick and you cannot go out, you have time to look deeply and spend some time with yourself. This may be one of the only times when you really lie down and spend some time coming home to yourself.

Even death is not exactly suffering. Death is also part of life. It's not the enemy. We know that many cells of our bodies are dying at every moment, so that new cells can be born. So death takes place all the time. Without death, birth isn't possible. Imagine there were no death. There would only be very old people walking around all over the planet, and no room for babies to be born! So we can work toward accepting death without fear. Death is something natural. Furthermore, if we look deeply, we see that we are not really dying; we will continue in other forms. Changing from one form to another may be something joyful.

CONTINUATION

Suppose you are a cloud. You can use this as an image for meditation. You are made of tiny crystals of ice or water. You are so light that you don't fall; you can float. There are huge clouds, millions of tons of water, floating around like that. There is interaction, collision, between these tiny crystals of ice. Some of the crystals may come together and form a big piece of ice, which as it descends becomes a large drop of water, and it falls as rain. But maybe halfway down, the drops encounter a mass of hot air, so you evaporate and you come up again; you go down; you come up, down and up. Transmigration, reincarnation, and rebirth are always taking place in the cloud. A cloud does not need to become rain in order to have a new life. A cloud has a new life every moment.

If you see a cloud floating in the sky and you think that it's always the same cloud, that's not true. A cloud is very active. A cloud can produce very powerful energy, such as lightning, which can cause destruction and move very quickly. There is a lot of cloud in us. We drink clouds every day when we drink water. Birth, death, and rebirth take place within us in the same way. Birth and death are taking place in every moment of our daily lives.

If someone asks you, "What happens to me when I die?" you may help that person by asking, "What is happening to you in the here and the now?" If we know what happens to us in the here and the now, we can answer the other question very easily. We are undergoing birth and death right now. Rebirth is taking place right now, because mentally and physically you are reborn every instant, you are renewed in every instant in order to become a new person, a new being. If we know how to do it, our renewal is beautiful.

We don't need to wait until we die in order to know what will happen to us. Looking deeply in the present moment, we see that birth and death are taking place in us at every moment, both in our bodies and in our consciousness. In every moment of our daily lives there is input and there is output. We breathe in; we take in food; and we have new ideas and new feelings. We breathe out, defecate, and let go of ideas and feelings. So air and water, the whole cosmos, is going through us, renewing us, and we are returning other things to the cosmos.

Suppose we speak of the death of a cloud. We look up in the sky and we don't see our beloved cloud anymore and we cry, "Oh my beloved cloud, you are no longer there. How can I survive without you?" We are thinking of the cloud as having passed from being into nonbeing, from existence into nonexistence. But in fact, it is impossible for a cloud to die. To die means from something you suddenly become nothing; from being someone you suddenly become no one. But this is not the case of the cloud. The cloud cannot become nothing. It is possible for a cloud to become rain, snow, fog, or water vapor. But it's not possible for a cloud to become nothing.

Your birth is not your beginning. It's only your continuation, because you were there before your birth, in other forms. For example, this page that you are reading existed first in many other forms. It didn't come from nothing, because from nothing you can't become something. Looking into the sheet of paper, we see the forest, the trees, the cloud, the rain, and the soil that nourishes the trees. We can see the saw that cut the tree down, the lumberjack, and the paper mill. The sheet of paper has not come from nothing. Its manifestation as a sheet of paper is only a new manifestation, not really a birth. So the nature of this sheet of paper is the nature of no birth and no death. It is impossible for the sheet of paper to die. When you burn the sheet of paper and you observe what happens, you see that the sheet of paper is transformed into smoke, vapor, ash, and heat. The heat is energy, which radiates; the smoke goes up into the air and becomes a cloud, and the ash falls down to the earth. The sheet of paper will continue. Like the cloud and like the sheet of paper, we continue, but in other forms.

Suppose one part of the cloud is able to transform itself into rain and it falls down and becomes part of the river. The rest of the cloud is up in the sky and, looking down, sees its continuation down below on Earth. It may think, "Have a good journey down there. I'll enjoy it up here, but you, who .in' part of me, I hope you enjoy it down there." To be floating up here is nice, but to be flowing down there is also nice. As a human being we can see that too. We can see ourselves in our children, our students, our friends, and our family. Their good luck is our good luck. Our happiness and suffering depend on them. We see ourselves everywhere, because every moment we produce thoughts, speech, and actions that continue us in the world.

SUFFERING DEPENDS ON OUR PERCEPTIONS

Much of our suffering depends on our perceptions. Whenever we don't get what we want, we see that as suffering. Of course if we don't get what we want, we suffer. But the truth is that sometimes we *do* get what we want and we suffer more. Maybe it's not what we thought it was, or it changes something else in our lives for the worse. Sometimes, after we get the thing we thought we wanted, we don't treasure it anymore; we want something else.

THE SECOND ARROW

Pain may be unavoidable. But whether you suffer or not is up to you. Suffering is optional; you choose to suffer or not to suffer. Birth, old age, and sickness are natural. It's possible not to suffer because of them when you have chosen to accept them as part of life. You may choose not to suffer, even if pain or sickness is there. How you see life and your particular situation depends on your way of looking.

If we look deeply into our suffering, we can ask ourselves what we have done, or are still doing, to contribute to it. That doesn't mean that our suffering isn't real, just that we can lessen it instead of adding to it and that we can even transform it.

The Buddha said that we should not amplify our pain by exaggerating the situation. He used the image of someone who is hit by an arrow. A few minutes later a second arrow strikes exactly the same spot. After the second arrow strikes, not only is the pain doubled, but it can be ten times more painful and intense. So when we have some pain, whether it is physical or mental, we can recognize it as suffering, but we don't need to exaggerate it. We can breathe with it:

Breathing in, I know that I am suffering.
Breathing out, I smile at my suffering.

We can very well make friends with our suffering as part of our effort to transform it. If we recognize it and call it by its true name, then we can make peace with it and not suffer us much. When we see the pain in the world caused by all the suffering, we want to help the world to suffer less. But we begin with ourselves. We have to produce peace in ourselves and reduce the suffering in ourselves first, because we represent the world. Peace, love, and happiness begin with mu selves. The suffering we see out in the world is reflected in the suffering, fear, and anger inside. So when we take care of ourselves, we are taking the first step toward taking care of the world.

NO MUD, NO LOTUS

Imagine there was no suffering. This is like trying to imagine a lotus growing without the mud that nurtures it. You can't plant lotus on marble. If there's no mud, there's no lotus. So if you want to have lotus flowers, you have to get some mud. If you look deeply into the nature of the lotus, you will see the mud in it. You don't need to look at the mud, you only need to look at the lotus and you will see the mud in it. You can't remove the mud from the lotus. If you tried to do so, the lotus would cease to be a lotus. Lotus flowers are made of non-lotus elements, including mud. Happiness is made of non-happiness elements, including suffering.

LEARNING FROM SUFFERING

Many people think of heaven as a place of pure bliss where there is no suffering. But the substance that makes happiness is understanding and love. In this world, we don't have enough understanding and love. We are thirsty for it. Sometimes we may feel sometimes that no one understands us or loves us. If people loved and understood us, we wouldn't need to wait for heaven. We could be happy on Earth right here and now. My definition of heaven is a place where there is plenty of understanding and compassion, and that implies that there is also suffering. If there's no suffering, then it's not a very good place to learn.

Many of us are afraid of ill-being, and our natural tendency is to try to run away from it. This has become a collective habit. There is an epidemic of medicating ourselves with alcohol, drugs, sedatives, and tranquilizers to escape our suffering. But the First

Noble Truth suggests that we should stay and acknowledge our suffering. If we don't understand suffering, we can't understand happiness.

Compassion and love are born from understanding. How can you love someone unless you understand their joy and pain? How can you love your child or your partner unless you understand their pain and challenges? If you want to love someone and make them happy, you can ask the question, "Do I understand my child enough?" "Do I understand my partner enough?" You can even go to your partner, your friend, or your child and ask, "Darling, do you think I understand you enough?" That person will tell you the answer.

What would happen if you said to your partner, "Darling, because I love you and want to make you happy, I want to understand you better. As a child, how did you suffer and what made you happy? Please tell me; help me. I know very well that if I don't understand you, I won't be able to be the best partner for you." That is the language of love.

Understanding requires understanding the difficulties, frustration, and pain of the person you love. If you have already understood your own pain, it will be much easier to understand the pain of the other person. If we understand the nature of the ill-being inside us, it will be much easier to understand the nature of the ill-being around us. The Buddha advises us not to try to run away from our own suffering, but to embrace it and look deeply into it. With deep looking, understanding will arise, and compassion will be born. Understanding and compassion make happiness possible.

STOPPING AND LOOKING DEEPLY

To begin to understand another person's suffering, we need to practice looking, listening, and observing our own suffering more deeply. The way to look deeply is to stop whatever rise we're doing and truly concentrate on what we're observing. This has two parts. The first is stopping, *shamatha* in Sanskrit. When you stop, your mind is very still, and you see things deeply. The second part is *vipashyana*, looking deeply. When you practice stopping, your mind sees things more clearly. Stopping and being in touch with what is positive, you become fresh. You nourish yourself with the food of the practice.

MERE RECOGNITION

When we stop, what are we stopping? We're stopping our minds. If you're walking mindfully or sitting mindfully, you continue to walk or sit, but you stop your mind and come back to the present moment with every step and with every breath. You stop focusing on your worries and anxieties and let them pass by. Of course these worries and anxieties will come back anyway, but you can just say "hello" and "good-bye" to them again. You don't need to force them away or fight them. You don't need to think, "Oh, it's terrible, I think about all that too much!" You just say "hello" and "bye-bye," gently like that. If your thoughts are strong, you may need to say this many times. Slowly your stopping will become more relaxed and effective.

CULTIVATING COMPASSION

We can learn a lot from suffering. Looking deeply into the nature of suffering will help us cultivate understanding and compassion. This is how we can talk about the "goodness of suffering." If we have suffered, that's good—then we have the materials to learn and the possibility of happiness. We make use of the suffering; it's with suffering that we can fabricate understanding and love. Handling suffering is an art. If you know how to handle your pain, your sorrow, and your fear, you know how to create happiness. The art of creating happiness and the art of handling suffering are same thing.

CALLING SUFFERING BY ITS TRUE NAMES

According to the First Noble Truth, we need to call our suffering by its true name. Once we have named what is causing us to suffer, we are more able to look deeply into each Pilfering in order to find a way to transform it. If we don't understand the nature of ill-being, we will be blind to the path leading to well-being. Looking into suffering, we discover the truth about how ill-being is made and what kind of path can lead to its transformation into well-being.

4

THE SECOND NOBLE TRUTH

THE IGNOBLE PATH

Once we have called our suffering by its true name, we need to look deeply to see where this suffering comes from. If we accept the first truth of suffering, we have to accept that there are causes for this suffering, because everything has its roots. When we look deeply into the roots and examine them, we have already begun to transform, our suffering. How has the ill-being come to be? We don't need to find the answer by trusting that Buddha or God created suffering for mysterious reasons. We only need to use our clear minds and our calm hearts to look deeply and see the causes. There are ways of perceiving and ways of living that lead to ill-being. This is the Second Noble Truth: the causes of suffering.

The Second Noble Truth can be conceived of as a path. But it's not a path that leads to happiness and well-being. It's a path leading to suffering. Many of us have taken the path that leads to anger, discrimination, violence, ignorance, and despair. The path of suffering is the ignoble path of wrong view, wrong thinking, wrong speech, wrong actions, wrong livelihood, wrong diligence, wrong mindfulness, and wrong concentration. If we understand how and why we've been walking the path of suffering, then we can see its opposite. The Noble Eightfold Path, the path to well-being, will reveal itself.

Why are we in the midst of economic crisis? Why is there so much pollution, terrorism, and climate change? When we ask these questions, we need to take the time and space to really look deeply to try to find the answer. No matter what our religious backgrounds, we have to acknowledge the true sufferings of our world and sit down together to try to find the causes.

Some Buddhist teachers say that desire is the basic cause of all ill-being. It's not true. Desire is only one tiny part of the wrong path. The real block of our suffering is caused by wrong view, which in turn leads to wrong thinking, and so on. The suffering of the world and our own suffering have been created by wrong views and wrong thinking. When we begin to see that we are creating our own suffering we can begin to see how we can transform it.

If we want to transform the situation of global warming, for example, we need to understand what is producing the carbon monoxide that is heating the Earth's surface. Coal burning power plants are the largest source of carbon dioxide pollution in the United States—they produce 2.5 billion tons every year. Automobiles, the second largest source, create nearly 1.5 billion tons of CO_2 annually.* We also have to look at what we consume every day that contributes to climate change. We drive cars, use electricity and gas, and destroy the forests in order to raise livestock to eat. All of these things contribute to global climate change. If we drive a lot, if we keep the lights on, if we eat too much meat, then the causes of our suffering accumulate.

If we look deeply into the Second Noble Truth, we not

---

*www.nrdc.org/globalwarming/fioi.asp

only see the ways we cause our own suffering, we see how to transform it. If we take care of ourselves and are less stressed, we cause less personal suffering, less irritation and conflict with our loved ones, and we're more likely to keep ourselves healthy. If we don't eat meat, farmers won't raise livestock to kill for our use. If we don't drive, we'll produce a lot less carbon monoxide. If we insist that large companies also stop polluting, we're actively doing something to create less suffering and more peace in the world.

THE FOUR NUTRIMENTS: OUR CONSUMPTION CAUSES OUR SUFFERING AND OUR JOY

What we consume is the cause of a lot of our suffering. The Buddha spoke of Four Nutriments, the four kinds of food that can bring us either well-being or ill-being. Happiness and suffering can be understood in terms of food, the nutrients we consume every day.

The Buddha said, "If you look deeply into the nature of what has come to be—namely your ill-being, your depression—and identify the source of the nutrients that have created it, you are already on the path of transformation and healing."

THE FIRST NUTRIMENT: EDIBLE FOOD

The first kind of nutriment is edible food, what we actually put into our mouths, chew, swallow, or drink. If it is good food, healthy food, then there will be no problem, there will be well-being. If it's not appropriate, then we can become ill. So before eating, we should look at the dishes on the table and breathe in and out to see whether that kind of food is good for us or not.

We can remove a dish that we think is not good for our health.

Mindful consumption of edible food also affects how we shop. Mindfully shopping at the grocery store or marketplace means you know what to buy and what not to buy. We can choose healthy food. Mindful consumption affects the way we cook. When we cook, we have another occasion to practice mindfulness. When we sit around the table to eat, we have another opportunity to be aware. We can eat in such a way that we reduce the suffering of living beings. Merely by the way we eat, we can help preserve our planet—if we know how to eat properly and in such a way that can help us cultivate compassion. We know that without compassion we can't be happy, because we can't relate to other living beings.

THE BUDDHA'S EXAMPLE: THE SON'S FLESH

To illustrate the first nutriment, edible food, the Buddha told the story of a young family who had to cross a desert. Halfway across, they ran out of food. After much thinking and debating, the parents decided to kill the little boy and eat his flesh to survive. After telling this story the Buddha asked the monks, "My dear friends, do you think that the couple enjoyed eating the flesh of their son?" The monks said, "No, dear teacher, it's not possible. No one can enjoy eating the flesh of their own son." The Buddha said, "When we eat, we should eat in such a way that can preserve compassion in us, otherwise it will be as though we are eating the flesh of our own sons."

When we eat without mindfulness, we may well be eating the flesh of our own sons or daughters. Over forty thousand children die every day because of the lack of food or the lack of nutrition.* Yet in many countries in the West people waste a tremendous amount of food. We use the cereal we grow to make alcohol and feed livestock. We want to eat chicken, pork, and beef, but in order to make a pound of meat we have to use ten to twenty times as much cereal. Yet the people in the world don't have enough grain, rice, and corn to eat. So when we look deeply at our piece of meat, we know that it has been made from huge amounts of grain that could have been used to save people who are dying from hunger and malnutrition.

Mindfulness helps us to see things that other people cannot see. That is why before eating we should look at our food to see whether eating it will harm our compassion or will help develop our compassion. The following meal contemplation can be very useful:

Let us eat in such a way that we keep our compassion alive, reduce the suffering of living beings, preserve our planet, and reverse the processes of global climate change.

THE SECOND NUTRIMENT: SENSORY IMPRESSION

The second kind of food is sensory impression. This kind of food isn't consumed with our mouths, but with our eyes, our ears, our noses, our bodies, and our minds. Depending on the content, consuming television, books, films, the Internet, and conversations can be either healthy or toxic.

Sometimes, we are suffering for other reasons, and we try to escape from our suffering with even more consumption, which brings more suffering. We are upset so we watch a television show, and then, depending on the content, we feel even more

---

* World Health Organization

upset. Sensory consumption also includes what we hear from others. If we listen to gossip, judgment, and insult, then we are consuming these things. If what we consume fills us with irritation, anger, or craving, then it creates more irritation, violence, and suffering in the world. We can have a strategy of mindful consumption so that what we read, watch, and listen to doesn't cause more suffering for ourselves and others.

THE BUDDHA'S EXAMPLE: THE COW WITH SKIN DISEASE

To illustrate how the wrong consumption of sensory impressions can lead to suffering, the Buddha used a very drastic image of a cow with practically no skin left as a result of disease, so it can easily be attacked by many kinds of microorganisms. When the cow lies down, the microorganisms from the soil come up and fix themselves on to the cow and suck its blood. When the cow is brought close to a tree or an ancient wall, the microorganisms in the bark of the tree or in the wood or stone of the wall will come out and suck the blood of the cow. The cow has no means to protect herself, because her skin is so thin.

In modern life, we are exposed to advertisements, violence, enticing programs, and images that try to incite our craving twenty-four hours a day. When we aren't mindful, we don't have a skin to protect us and what we see and hear penetrates and assaults us. Without mindfulness, we have no means to protect ourselves and we suffer.

When we drive through the city, we are consuming—whether we want to or not. Advertisements penetrate our consciousness and the consciousness of our children, who less able to filter these sources of toxic consumption.

LIVING WITHOUT TELEVISION

I remember one day a little boy came to Plum Village, the retreat center where I live, and he wanted to leave right away, because there was no television. He believed that it wasn't possible for him to survive without television. He looked at the schedule: sitting meditation, mindful breakfast, and walking meditation and said, "This is like a military camp." So one of the nuns said to him, "Okay, we'll bring you to the railway station to go home. But you have to wait a few hours, because the next train doesn't leave until seven in the evening. Meanwhile, a group of young people came and invited him to play with them. When the time came to go to the railway station, he said, "Well, I can stay another day." And finally he stayed for two weeks. When the time came for him to go home, he told his mother, "Why do we have to go?" He found he could survive very well without television and had discovered that there were other things that could nourish him much better. We may feel like we can't live without consuming certain sensory impressions. But if we try, if we have the space, the opportunity, and the supportive environment to consume healthy nutriments, our suffering diminishes.

THE THIRD NUTRIMENT: VOLITION

The third kind of nutriment is volition, also called aspiration or desire. Every one of us has a deep desire inside, and this desire is a nutriment. If we didn't have any desire at all, we wouldn't care about living. We wouldn't have any energy. Everyone has a true and deep desire. The desire itself can be healthy or toxic and can cause well-being or suffering. When Siddhartha left his palace to become a monk, he had the desire to practice and to be enlightened in order to help people to suffer less. This is a wholesome desire, a good nutriment, because this food gave him a lot of energy to overcome difficulties and succeed in his aspiration. But there are other kinds of desires, like the desire to kill or to punish, which are toxic.

Compassion is a positive energy. If you are a social worker, you may want to help children in the developing world who are dying from malnutrition. If you volunteer to go and help, it means you accept living a simple life. You are able to do so because you have the strength of a wholesome desire. Each of us can look to see if we can recognize our deepest desire, whether it is healthy or not, and whether it is bringing us suffering or happiness, because that is the food that nourishes our lives.

THE BUDDHA'S EXAMPLE: WE ARE DRAGGED BY TWO STRONG MEN

To illustrate the third nutriment, the Buddha used the image of two strong men dragging a third man toward a pit of glowing embers. The young man they are dragging doesn't want to die. So the two strong men represent that kind of negative volition within us that is very strong, but that only brings us more suffering. Examples of toxic volition are the craving for sex, fame, wealth, revenge, and causing others to suffer. If you are motivated by that kind of desire, it's as if the desire has abducted you and you are being pulled in the direction of death.

THE FOURTH NUTRIMENT: CONSCIOUSNESS

The fourth kind of nutriment is collective consciousness. We are influenced by the ways of thinking of the people around us, and we consume the views of other people in many ways. Individual consciousness is made of collective consciousness, and collective consciousness is made of individual consciousness. It is our consciousness that designs our world.

THE BUDDHA'S EXAMPLE: BEING STABBED ONE HUNDRED TIMES

To illustrate this nutriment, the Buddha uses the example of a criminal who has been caught and is brought before the king. The king orders that the criminal is to be executed by being stabbed one hundred times. But the next morning, after being stabbed, the criminal doesn't die. So the king orders that at noon the criminal be executed by being stabbed again one hundred times. But still the criminal doesn't die. So the king orders him to be executed that evening by being slabbed one hundred times more. The wounds inflicted by the collective consciousness can be as painful as those stab wounds. Taking in toxins from the environment can be like being stabbed hundreds of times.

If we live in an environment where people around us are very angry, violent, and cruel, then sooner or later we'll become angry and cruel like them. This happens even if we don't want it to, because we—and especially our children—are continuously influenced and penetrated by the collective consciousness of our environment.

ORIGINAL FEAR: ONE SOURCE OF OUR SUFFERING

Why do we continue to consume toxic nutriments if they only bring us more suffering? Partly it's because we still have a lot of original fear inside from the time we were small children. By consuming in order to distract ourselves from that original suffering, we create more suffering. As newborns, we were very vulnerable. We knew we couldn't survive on our own. We call that original fear.

There are those of us who are depressed and continue to suffer even when in the present situation everything looks all right. We have a tendency to go home to the past. We feel more comfortable in that home in the past, even if in that home there is a lot of suffering. We return again and again to the past, because our original suffering and fear have not been relieved.

Suppose you're a boatperson who has crossed the ocean and arrived safely and been accepted in another country. You're safe; you have a job; but you've still kept a picture of the ocean you crossed as a boatperson in your mind. While crossing the ocean you could have drowned at any time or been devoured by sharks. Crossing the ocean is very risky, and hundreds of thousands of boatpeople have died at sea. So you still have that memory; you still have that picture in your mind. Every time you imagine that ocean, you suffer. But it is only a picture. You can drown and die in the ocean, but not in a picture.

THE TEN FETTERS THAT BIND US

Our suffering comes primarily from our minds and how we see the world. In the Buddhist tradition we speak of the ten Muds of fetters, *samyojana,* that bind us and deprive us of our freedom. The Sanskrit word samyojana can be translated as "knots" and these fetters are like tight knots inside us. These fetters push us to do and say things that we don't want to do and say. They're very powerful. Our mindfulness, concentration, and insight must also be powerful to untie these knots.

THE FIRST FETTER: CRAVING

The first fetter is craving. The danger of craving is that we believe that the object of our craving is what we really want, that it is what can truly bring us happiness. So we don't see the danger of running after the object of our craving. But when craving arises in us, we're no longer at peace. We're not satisfied with what we have and who we are.

The teaching of the Buddha is about living happily right now in the present. But when the flame of craving is inside us, we no longer have the capacity to do that. We believe that without the object of our craving we can't be really happy, so we lose all our peace and the capacity to be happy in the here and now. How can we undo this fetter?

The Buddha used many images to illustrate craving. One is that the person who has craving is like someone holding a torch and going against the wind; the fire will burn his hand. The second image the Buddha spoke of is that of a dog chewing on a bare bone. No matter how much he chews on the bone, he will never be satisfied, because on the bone there's no meat, no juice left. Nowadays the bone may be made of plastic. The object of craving is like that. It can never satisfy us.

The third image is that of a hook and bait that's used to catch fish. You throw the baited hook into the river. When the fish sees the bait it looks so appealing and he wants to bite it. But the fish doesn't know that inside the bait there is a hook. The object of our craving is like that; the danger is hidden. Sometimes the bait is made of plastic and the fish can't even eat it. Nevertheless, it looks very appealing and the fish bites it and gets hooked. So we have to look deeply in order to see the true nature of the object of our craving. If we see it clearly, it will lose its appeal and then we will be free. That's why we need to look deeply to see the hidden dangers of the objects of our craving.

THE SECOND FETTER: ANGER

The second fetter is anger and violence. The flame of anger is as destructive as the flame of craving. When anger inhabits us, we have no peace, no capacity to be happy in the here and now. We have to practice concentration, looking deeply, in order to see that our anger arises from ignorance and wrong views. Understanding the First and Second Noble Truths—suffering and its causes—we will be able to overcome our anger and untie the knots of anger. If we feel anger arising in us, we can practice stopping and breathing in such a way that we can untie the knot of our anger.

THE THIRD FETTER: IGNORANCE

The third fetter is ignorance. Ignorance means wrong view. We are confused and we don't know where to go and what to do. So from our ignorance, we do and say the wrong things. We don't know what's right and wrong and, instead of sitting with our ignorance and letting insight arise, we act out of ignorance. That is the third kind of fetter we have to undo.

THE FOURTH FETTER: COMPLEXES

The fourth fetter is our complexes that cause us to spend our time and energy comparing ourselves to others. There are three complexes: superiority, inferiority, and equality. Each of these binds us, even the equality complex, because we are Incused on a sense of self versus other, and we're competing and comparing ourselves with other people. These complexes exist because we have the notion that we are a separate self. We compare that self with the other selves. That is how the three complexes arise, and they only bring suffering.

THE FIFTH FETTER: DOUBT

The fifth fetter is doubt and suspicion. When we have suspicion or doubt in us, we're not at peace, we're not free. Our suspicion and doubt may come from our ignorance, our complexes, or our craving. Perhaps we know what is right, but we don't act on it, because we are held back by our doubts and suspicions.

THE SIXTH FETTER (THE FIRST VIEW): THIS BODY IS ME

The sixth through the tenth fetters focus on the wrong perceptions and wrong views that lead to our suffering. The sixth fetter is the view that this body is me, that this body is a separate self. You simply believe that you *are* this body. That means you think that with the disintegration of this body you will no longer be here. You believe that before the formation of this body you were not here. If you have this view, than you add so much unnecessary suffering to your life.

THE SEVENTH FETTER (THE SECOND VIEW): PAIRS OF OPPOSITES

The second view is to believe that pairs of opposites are unrelated. You believe that right is totally other than left, that there is birth and there is death, that there is inside and outside, being and nonbeing, and sameness and otherness. All these concepts form pairs of opposites. To be caught in them is to have wrong view. The teaching of the Buddha helps us to transcend pairs of opposites in order for us to come to a view that is free from dualistic thinking. The Middle Way is the way of nonduality. It transcends all pairs of opposites, including being and nonbeing, birth and death, inside and outside, and object and subject.

THE EIGHTH FETTER (THE THIRD VIEW): ATTACHMENT TO VIEWS

When you learn about something, you form a notion about it. This is very natural. But if you're then caught by that notion, you don't let in new information or ideas to change that notion. You cannot progress on your spiritual path. So whatever you have learned, whatever you have heard, you should be careful not to consider it to be the absolute truth. You should be able to let it go in order to arrive at a higher truth. In science, if you've discovered something and you believe it to be the ultimate truth, then you won't search anymore, and you're no longer a true scientist.

In order to progress on our path, we have to be ready to release our view, release our understanding. It's like climbing a ladder. If you've come up to the fourth rung, and you think that you are on the highest rung, then you won't climb any higher. You have to release the fourth rung in order to get to the fifth. And when you've reached the fifth, you should be ready to release it in order to get to the sixth. So knowledge can be an obstacle to wisdom. If you see and understand something, be sure that it's something you'll be able to release in the future in order to get to a higher kind of truth. That is the teaching on nonattachment to views.

THE NINTH FETTER (THE FOURTH VIEW): PERVERTED VIEW

Suppose you believe that things just happen by chance and that there's no cause and effect. That is a kind of perverted view. The law of cause and effect means that when you sow a bean seed, you will harvest beans. When you sow a seed of anger, you will harvest anger. If you're caught by the fetter of perverted view, you don't understand why things happen. They just strike you as unfair or capricious, because you don't believe in the law of cause and effect; you think that everything happens just by chance. When you're able to observe something deeply, you can see that it manifests because of many conditions coming together. Believing that there is only one cause is a perverted view. Of course, we all experience hurt, illness, and pain that we cannot control. But much of the additional suffering we experience on top of this pain is caused by perverted view. The Four Noble Truths teach us that our additional suffering often comes from a way of living that is full of wrong perceptions, wrong thinking, wrong speech, and wrong action.

THE TENTH FETTER (THE FIFTH VIEW): ATTACHMENT TO RITES AND RITUALS

When you believe that by performing a particular rite or ritual you can experience liberation and salvation, then you're caught by rites and rituals. Perhaps you believe that you can eat every kind of meat except beef, and that eating beef will prevent your salvation. Or you believe that you can eat every kind of meat except pork. That is the kind of taboo or precept that you can get caught in. With understanding you can liberate yourself. It's not by performing rituals and ceremonies and observing taboos that you can become liberated. There is not one action or one ritual that will bring you liberation. Liberation requires continual practice, continual commitment to mindfulness, concentration, and insight.

To illustrate this fetter, I sometimes use the example of someone bowing to the Buddha on the altar. The right practice of bowing is a kind of meditation, a way of looking deeply. That is why before bowing to the Buddha you should know that the Buddha is in you and you are in the Buddha, both of you, the Buddha and you, have the nature of emptiness. This is a way of looking deeply, and it has the power of liberating us. If we don't do this, and we believe that bowing to the Buddha is an act of devotion that will help us to be saved, we are caught in rituals.

Performing the Eucharist is the same. The priest breaks the bread and gives it to you, and he gives you the wine to drink. If, when you eat the bread and drink the wine, you are in touch with the whole cosmos, then you are not caught in the ritual, because in the piece of bread you see that the sunshine, the clouds, the earth, and everything in the whole cosmos is in the bread. When the priest performs the Eucharist, he wants you to be alive and in touch with Jesus Christ as a reality in you. To automatically perform the ritual is to be caught in the ritual. Then we don't get anything except the ritual. Real communion is possible when you are truly alive as you participate in the ritual. That is what you want, not just a performance of an empty form. The same thing is true in every tradition.

Walking meditation or sitting meditation can be just a ritual. Chanting can be just a ritual. We get caught in rituals so easily, and that's one of the fetters we have to break through. If we practice wholeheartedly, not just following the rote practice, then the practice of mindfulness and insight will liberate us, and rites and rituals will become a vehicle and an opportunity to practice.

UNDERSTANDING THE CAUSES OF ILL-BEING LEADS TO HAPPINESS

The Second Noble Truth reminds us that once we have called suffering by its true name, we need to look deeply to see and gather its causes. We don't need to look to a god to tell us why people suffer. We can see the causes of suffering by using our own clear minds, our own deep insight. Only then can we move to the Third Noble Truth: well-being and the transformation of suffering.

5

THE THIRD NOBLE TRUTH

HAPPINESS IS POSSIBLE

Once we understand the causes of our suffering, we can see that transforming them will lead to the cessation of ill-being, namely to well-being. If there is ill-being, the opposite of ill-being is there at the same time. It's like the left and the right. When you confirm the existence of ill-being, you confirm the existence of something else, which is well-being. Well-being cannot be there without ill-being and vice versa. The cessation of suffering and the existence of well-being is the Third Noble Truth. When the roots of suffering are absent, we can be free and happy, and we can act ethically, motivated by our understanding and compassion.

WELL-BEING AND ILL-BEING

Well-being is the cessation of ill-being, just as light is the cessation of darkness. Ill-being is there. That is the First Noble Truth. We know that something unpleasant produces ill-being. But we also know that something pleasant can produce ill-being as well. For example, falling in love can bring suffering in its wake.

Sometimes, we only see the ill-being. We see the garbage or the mud, but we miss the lotus that grows in it. The Third Noble Truth reminds us that not only ill-being but also well-being is there. Because of the cessation of ill-being, there is the presence of well-being. The cessation of ill-being means the presence of well-being. The Third Noble Truth confirms the existence, the possibility, of well-being.

The Third Noble Truth reminds us that it is possible to live happily in the present moment. It is an affirmation that ill-being can be transformed. There is a path that leads to happiness and we need to learn that path.

The Third Noble Truth is based on the understanding that each of us has Buddha nature, *buddhata,* the seed of a Buddha inside us. We all have the ability to be mindful, to be concentrated, and to have deep insight.

WATERING THE SEEDS

According to Buddhist psychology, inside every human being are the seeds of all the various mental formations. We have the seeds of compassion and loving kindness in us. We also have the seeds of craving and violence. What seeds manifest depends in large part on what seeds were watered in our childhoods and by our ancestors. It's like a stream of running water. If you dig a canal that slopes to the west, the stream will flow to the west. If you dig a canal that slopes to the east, the water will flow to the east. We can learn how to dig the canal to go in the direction of happiness and well-being.

HAPPINESS IS RELATIVE

Despite all the suffering in the world, we each also have many opportunities for happiness. When we water the seeds of mindfulness through practice, happiness will appear. The other morning when I opened my water tap to wash my face, I felt my fingers as they were in touch with the water. I felt that the water was very fresh. The water had either come from a very deep source in the earth or from high mountains, and it was connected to the water tap in my room. Outside it was very cold, so the water inside was also very cold, and when I wet my eyes it was so refreshing, like the Buddha's teaching. Whenever I brush my teeth I do so aware that I am free from all agitation, worries, and projects. I dwell peacefully, freely, happily in the present moment, in touch with what is positive, like the cool fresh water. My eyes are still in good condition and my legs still let me walk. I'm very happy.

So our happiness is very relative. If you have more mindfulness, then your happiness increases. Because you're aware of the positive elements in your life, you're happier. But if you're not mindful, if you're carried away by your worries, your irritation, or your fear, then you won't be happy in that moment.

FINDING HAPPINESS IN THE PRESENT MOMENT

Suppose you are concerned about your health. Perhaps you're ill and you keep thinking about the past when you were healthier. Maybe you keep thinking about the future and imagining the situation might get worse. When you do this, your energy is dispersed. If you're concerned about your health, and if you're putting your energy into worrying, and you don't know what to do, then what you should do is go home to the present moment. When you go home to the present moment, you have the chance to get the insight and the wisdom to know what you should do and what you should not do. You will have more insight into what will improve the situation.

When you go home to the present moment, you see that there is worry and tension in you—tension in your body and worry in your mind. You know that this is not good for your healing. When you go home to yourself, you have an opportunity to find out that there are things you can do right away to help you take steps in the direction of healing and transformation. Relaxing your body and stopping the tension and worry are concrete things you can do right away. As practitioners we know how to do that. We know how to breathe in mindfully and allow our breathing to flow naturally. We know that breathing in and out can be very enjoyable.

Some people say, "Oh, I know the present moment; it's very boring." These people are used to being caught in the past and living in the world of memory. That's because they don't have the habit of being in the present moment. They're used to living in the past, and they consider the past to be their home. They're always sliding back to the past, worrying about the worries of the past, becoming fearful based on what made them fearful in the past, and so on. They have the impression that the past is their home; they're used to it, so they feel more at home in the past. Or they dream about the future, anticipating things that may happen. When they say the present moment is boring, it means they've never really been in the present moment. But the present is life. It's a whole world to discover. Your body is here in the present moment; your life is here in the present moment;

and the world is here in the present moment. That's why it's so important that we come home to the present moment—in order to truly live our lives.

MINDFUL WALKING

The practice of mindful walking can release the tension in your body. If you're really concentrated on your steps, you're fully established in the here and the now, and you are aware ill the wonders of life that are ready to nourish and support you. You are in touch with life and you are advancing on the path of healing.

Breathing in, I'm aware of the tension in my body.
Breathing out, I release all the tension in my body.

When you breathe in this way, you are already doing something for your healing.

When you're caught by the past, you can't do anything for yourself. When you're pulled away by the future, by your tears and worries, you can't do anything either. So go into the present moment, and you'll find out that there are things you can do right here and right now to facilitate your healing. You'll know what to eat and what not to eat for your health; you'll know which friend can help you with your difficulty. You can make a decision in the direction of healing: "I am determined not to eat that anymore, not to drink that anymore, not to smoke that anymore." In the present moment we have insight, and we know what to do and what not to do, and what resources are available in the here and now. That's why our practice is to always go home to the present moment where we can encounter all the wonders of life that have the power to refresh, nourish, and heal.

If you want to look for happiness, go back to the present moment. The present moment is the only door to happiness and well-being. When you go back to the present moment, you find out that there are so many conditions of happiness available. You can be happy right here, right now. The question is whether you are capable of being happy. You seek happiness, but maybe when happiness arrives, you're not capable of being happy.

Suppose you're a child walking by a bakery. You see so many delicious things inside and you hope that you can have one of those delicious-looking cakes. If your mother would buy you one, you'd be so happy. In your child mind, maybe you hope that someday you'll be free to enter a bakery like that and eat anything you like. Imagine the owner of the shop is inviting you in and saying, "My dear child, you can have anything you want. The whole shop is for you." I don't know how you'd react with so many wonderful, delicious things to eat. Maybe you'd be confused. You might not know where to begin. You might try one, but if you ate it too quickly, you wouldn't be able to eat more.

When we go home to the present moment, we may feel like that. There are so many wonderful things, so many conditions of happiness available, that we don't know what to do. We can begin with mindful breathing, mindful walking and movement, and allowing ourselves to be in touch with nature, to see whether we can handle the beauty and the happiness that life gives us.

It's very important to learn how to take a step in mindfulness, in freedom and ease; it can bring you a lot of healing and transformation, a lot of freedom and joy. You are welcome to make not just one step, but two, three, or four steps. And you'll be overwhelmed by happiness. It's very important that we cultivate our capacity of being happy. Happiness is only available here in the present moment. And you'll find that there are many more conditions of happiness than you thought.

MINDFULNESS, CONCENTRATION, AND INSIGHT ARE THE SOURCES OF HAPPINESS

If we are mindful of something, then we naturally begin to concentrate on it. Our concentration increases the quality of happiness. Suppose you have a good cup of tea. If you're mindful, you can concentrate on your tea. Your tea becomes something very real. The time of tea-drinking makes you so happy, because you are not disturbed. Your mind is not in the past, the future, or lost on your projects. The tea is the object of your concentration. That's why drinking tea in that moment can make you very happy. The more you are concentrated, the happier you become. We are used to thinking ill money and power as sources of happiness. But we already have many true sources of happiness in us that we don't know how to enjoy.

When you are mindful and concentrated, insight arises. You don't need to force it. When you have insight you can be very happy, because insight always liberates you. If you are inhabited by fear, you cannot be happy or joyful. If you are inhabited by worries, desire, or craving, you can't be peaceful; you can't be happy. But when you have insight, fear and craving are removed and true happiness comes to you.

HOME IS HERE AND NOW

When I look outside there's a bamboo grove on my left, and a forest and vineyard on my right, and I feel very clearly that I'm home. Our home is not in our memories; it's not a path leading to our old elementary school, or the blossoming of a tree from childhood. Those are memories. If you live in the present moment deeply, you create a new homeland in a very profound way. The autumn leaf is very beautiful, but the fresh green leaf of spring is also beautiful, and the deep green leaf of summer is beautiful too.

In the present moment, if you see things deeper, more profoundly, you see the richness and beauty of each tree. If you only see superficially, you might complain when it rains. But when you see deeply, you see the rain is wonderful, refreshing the earth, bringing us more water in the dry summer, and so on. Looking deeply, we enjoy everything, and we feel that life is enjoyable. You have more peace, and you think of the many positive conditions you have. Now that you have some happiness and solidity, you can turn to your difficulty and try to undo the difficulty. Usually we don't pay attention to what happens in the present moment. It's not until we're about to leave a place or a moment, that we regret not having been truly present.

SAMTUSTA: WE ALREADY HAVE ENOUGH

The Buddha spoke of *samtusta,* which means that you are satisfied with the conditions of life that you have. You already have enough conditions to be happy, and it is thanks to your mindfulness that you don't need more. It is possible to feel that what you have is sufficient and you do not need anything else. If you have mindfulness, if you feel safe, you recognize that you have plenty of conditions to be happy already, and that you don't need to run into the future in order to get a few more conditions. We've seen many people without diplomas who are very happy. We've seen many people who don't have a big house or a big car, and they are perfectly happy. Even if they manage to get the object of their desire, they may not be happy and will want to run after another one.

Samtusta has sometimes been translated as the awareness that you are satisfied with little. When you go home to the present moment and you review all the conditions of happiness that you already have, you may find they are more than enough for you to be happy right now.

Samtusta, non-craving, may be difficult to understand at first, but if we practice observing and naming what we see in us and around us, it becomes clear. This understanding is an essential part of the basis for a global ethic. We see many people who have plenty of money, plenty of power, but who suffer very deeply. These people have stress, loneliness, craving, and addiction. We only need to look around and see with our own eyes that power, money, and desire are not the answer. We don't need anyone to tell us this; we don't need to take a leap of faith to believe this. We can simply look around.

FOUR PRACTICES FOR LIVING HAPPILY IN THE PRESENT MOMENT

We can be happy right here and right now. The first practice is our awareness of the present moment. The second practice is the contemplation on the interbeing nature of pairs of opposites, such as being and nonbeing, suffering and happiness, and birth and death. The third practice is to make a great vow to ourselves, the vow of a bodhisattva, to transform our suffering and help others to do the same. The fourth practice is to practice mindful consumption. The Second Noble Truth explores the Four Nutriments and how what we consume affects our happiness and our suffering. We can choose to consume only food, sounds, sights, and environments that increase our happiness and we can avoid those that cause suffering. We can choose to eat healthy food, focus our awareness on beautiful sights, listen deeply to those who use loving speech, and make a concentrated effort to be around those who bring us more happiness.

FINDING OUR PATH TO HAPPINESS

Each of us has the capacity not only for great happiness but also for bringing great happiness to others. Each of us has Buddha nature. If we practice the ways of living happily in the present moment, we will water the seed of Buddha nature within us and help it to grow. If Buddha has seen the path to well-being and happiness, it is because he touched this wisdom within himself. We need to do the same. We can't seek to receive the path from anyone else. In order to touch the seeds of wisdom within us, all we need to do is practice sitting, walking, listening, and acting with mindful awareness. If we are able to walk together on this path, it is because of our own practice, not because of something laid down by a god or a rule of law.

6

THE FOURTH NOBLE TRUTH

AN ETHICAL WAY OF LIFE

The Second Noble Truth shows us the way of living that leads to suffering. But the Third Noble Truth reminds us that well-being and happiness are possible. There is a way of living ethically that can lead us out of our suffering. Only if we live ethically can we experience happiness and well-being. This way is the Noble Eightfold Path, the Fourth Noble Truth. It is the path leading to well-being and it is also the path of ethics. The two cannot be separated. Because of the nature of interbeing, there is no true wellbeing that does not consider the well-being of others.

The Eightfold Path consists of eight guidelines on how we can be in the world. The Eightfold Path guides us to perceive, think, arid act in a way that both brings us happiness and creates more happiness in the world. There is no difference between the two. The eight aspects of the Eightfold Path are: Right View, Right Thinking, Right Speech, Right Action, Right Livelihood, Right Diligence, Right Mindfulness, and Right Concentration.

HOW DO WE KNOW WHAT IS "RIGHT"?

What do we mean by "right"? Everyone wants Right Thinking, but what is it? We need mindful breathing, mindful sitting, mindful reflecting, in order to bring about Right Thinking and Right Speech. It must *truly* be Right Thinking, because our thinking might be wrong, yet we think it's right. During World War Two, the decision to drop the atomic bomb was thought to be Right thinking. But was it?

How should we think in order for our thinking to be right? What is Right Speech? What kind of speech makes our words Right Speech? By "right," to Buddha meant moral and ethical. Morality and ethics can be code of conduct that we would like to accept and follow. There are five sets of criteria that can help us judge whether something is right or wrong.

THE FIRST SET OF CRITERIA: SUFFERING AND HAPPINESS

The first set of criteria for determining right and wrong is whether something brings suffering or happiness. Whatever brings suffering is wrong. Whatever can bring happiness is right. That is one set of criteria, dukkha and sukha. But to use this set of criteria, we have to remember that there is a difference between suffering and pain. Because pain can be unavoidable, but that doesn't mean we have to suffer.

For example, separation can be painful, but if you're animated by a strong ideal, a strong vocation, or a strong aspiration, you can accept separation in order to realize your aspiration. When Siddhartha left home, he had to leave behind his wife, his child, his family, everything, in order to accept the hard life of an ascetic. You might be able to accept leaving your family and the comfort of your daily life in order to engage in a harder kind of life because you want to realize something important. This will ease the pain of separation. There is separation, but there is no suffering.

Suffering is not a simple thing. Sometimes pain is only pain, and when you are able to accept pain, you don't suffer. So there must be some difference between pain or lack of comfort on the one hand and suffering on the other.

Happiness is also not always a simple thing. There is a difference between happiness and pleasure just as there is a difference between pain and suffering. Many of us regard pleasure as happiness. If you inject a dose of heroin into your body, you feel pleasure. But there are those of us who don't see it as happiness. Some of us feel we're very happy drinking a lot of alcohol. There's a feeling of pleasure. But is it truly happiness? So pleasure may be different than happiness. There are kinds of pleasure that look like happiness. That's why we have to look more deeply. Pain is not exactly suffering; it can't be identified with suffering. And pleasure is different from happiness; it's not exactly the same as happiness.

Suppose you like hiking and you go hiking for the whole day. You climb and climb, you get hot, and you get scratches. You seem to suffer during hiking. There are people who prefer to stay home and watch television instead of going hiking. But if you are climbing and enjoying being on the mountain, perhaps when you think of those who are in their living rooms watching television, one program after another, you may feel sorry for them. So who is happy, the hiker or the television watcher? It depends.

Some consider going to school to be unpleasant, and they suffer. But there are children and young people who love to study and who find happiness in their studies. So whether going to school is dukkha or sukha depends on you. It's very hard to use this criterion of happiness or suffering to define whether going to school is right or wrong. So this set of criteria isn't enough.

THE SECOND SET OF CRITERIA: BENEFICIAL AND UNBENEFICIAL

The Four Noble Truths could be understood as saying that everything that leads to suffering is wrong, and everything that leads to the cessation of suffering is right. But we have to look more deeply into the nature of happiness and suffering in order to better understand. That is why we have another set of criteria, called "beneficial and unbeneficial" or what brings well-being as opposed to that which is harmful. Whatever is beneficial to you, to your health, your understanding, or your learning, is good. And what is not beneficial is bad, is wrong. Getting an education is beneficial. So this second set of criteria could support going to school and learning. When you drink alcohol, you get plea sure. But you know that drinking too much alcohol will harm you, is not beneficial. So this set of criteria can help you to see more clearly.

There are mental formations we describe as beneficial, like joy, compassion, forgiveness, understanding, and love. Every time you touch the seed of compassion, joy, or brotherhood in you, it will manifest as a mental formation and make you happy. This kind of practice helps develop your joy and happiness. These beneficial mental formations are also in your loved ones. So there are ways that you can help another person by touching these beneficial things in him or her so that these beneficial formations will manifest and make that person happy. And if that other person is happy, you will profit. So according to this set of criteria, what is beneficial and what is not beneficial determines what is right and what is wrong.

THE THIRD SET OF CRITERIA: DELUDED OR AWAKE

There is another set of criteria we can use based on whether you are deluded or awake. When your mind isn't clear you're not awake; you have wrong judgment; you make the wrong decision; and you do the wrong thing. Suppose you're under the influence of drugs or alcohol. You will not be clear-sighted; you will easily be deluded; and whatever decision you make in that moment cannot be right.

Suppose you're very angry with your child. In that moment your anger makes you not lucid, not clear. If in such a moment you write a document saying that you don't want your child to benefit from your inheritance, your decision will not be right. Don't do anything when you're not awake and clear-minded. Wait until you're yourself and quite awake before you make a decision. Deluded and awake is a set of criteria that can help determine what is right and what is wrong.

THE FOURTH SET OF CRITERIA: TO OPEN OR TO BAR THE WAY

Another set of criteria we need is knowing when to open up and when to bar the way. To open means sometimes you need to make an exception. Suppose you don't want to lie. You believe that telling the truth is always a good thing to do and that telling a lie is always wrong. But suppose someone is looking for a particular person in order to kill him, and he comes to ask you whether you've seen that person and where he is hiding. If you tell the truth, the other person will be killed. So you are forced to tell a lie, "No I haven't seen him." You're motivated by compassion and you open, you allow yourself to lie and make an exception. Morality without that kind of mental dexterity and flexibility would not be intelligent. That is why to open, to make an exception, to allow, is a very important thing to do.

Does the physician have the right to tell a lie to his patient? You are supposed to tell others the truth. But there are many ways of telling the truth. If you don't tell the truth at the right time, in the right place, the other person could die from hearing it. That's why you choose a good time to tell him, so he can receive the truth without having too big a shock. So how to decide whether or not to tell the truth, and how to tell the truth in a skillful way, is something a doctor should learn. Sometimes we choose not to tell the truth in order to help the other person to survive. So it's not simple; it's quite complicated. That's why we need deep understanding to be able to practice opening the door and making exceptions.

To bar the way means that sometimes, even when something isn't inherently wrong, you have to refrain from doing it. Suppose you drink a glass of wine every weekend. It gives you pleasure to drink an occasional glass of wine and in the last thirty years it hasn't damaged your body and you've never gotten drunk. Now you come to a retreat and people advise you to refrain from drinking alcohol completely. So you ask the question, "Why?" since it hasn't done you any harm. Why do you have to deprive yourself of this pleasure?

A lady in England once asked me that question. She said, "Why do I need to stop drinking my glass of wine? It's my pleasure." I told her, "Well, I know that you're perfectly right when you say it hasn't done you any harm. But children tend to do as their parents do. If parents smoke, the children are likely to smoke. Perhaps you don't have the seed of alcoholism in you, but one of your children may have it. To stop drinking is to support your children. It's not for your sake but for your children's sake." That's what it means to bar the way; we want to prevent a harmful thing that may happen in the future.

We are supposed to drink with moderation. But the fact is that if you don't take the first glass you never risk taking a second or a third glass. So refraining from taking the first glass is to bar the way. You yourself may do something and never get harmed at all. But your younger sibling may do the same thing and be harmed.

Someone who drinks alcohol and then drives home and gets there safely is very lucky. If he says, "I've been drinking and I'm all right," he doesn't realize he's just been lucky. So to not drink alcohol before you drive is to bar the way, to set an obstacle before you so that the harm and suffering can't happen.

THE FIFTH SET OF CRITERIA: APPEARANCE AND SUBSTANCE

The final set of criteria is appearance and substance. Sometimes it doesn't look like we're transgressing an ethical guideline when in fact we are. Suppose you're in a place where someone is trying to kill someone else and you have the capacity to intervene and prevent the damage but you don't do it. Although you're not a killer, you're violating the precept not to kill. You're not killing directly, but you allow the killing to take place. This is called "nonintervention." You don't intervene, and this is as much an action as acting to cause harm. You are still responsible for your actions. When you see a situation like that, you should intervene. You can't say, "Well, I am not responsible, it wasn't me who was doing the killing." But you were there, and you didn't intervene. You are responsible.

Sometimes we're forced to lie in order to save a life. If we don't lie it's a transgression. On the level of appearance, not to lie is the right thing. But in terms of substance, not to lie is wrong, because if you don't lie, the other person will die. This is an important set of criteria. On the level of appearance it looks right, but in terms of its content and context, it's wrong. Sometimes you have to lie. And sometimes you have to kill. It's very difficult. Applied ethics is a discipline that studies how a moral outcome can be obtained in specific circumstances. We don't just speculate whether something is right or wrong. We have to question the norms that have been set up to see if our behavior is truly ethical.

We can use these ethical criteria in daily life. Ultimately, we work to transcend all criteria and norms. Buddhist ethical philosophy can be summed up in the following terms.

Both subject and object of perception manifest from consciousness according to the principle of interbeing. Humans are present in all things, and all things are present in humans. On the phenomenal level, there seems to be birth and death, being and nonbeing. But ontologically, these notions cannot be applied to reality. The dynamic consciousness is called karma energy. Everything evolves according to the principle of interdependence. But there is free will and the possibility to transform. There is probability. The one affects the all. And the all affects the one. Interbeing also means impermanence, nonself, emptiness, karma, and countless world systems. Right View allows Right Action, leading to the reduction of suffering and the increase of happiness. Happiness and suffering inter-are. The ultimate reality transcends notions of good and evil, right and wrong.

AN EXAMPLE OF USING THE CRITERIA: THE ATOMIC BOMB

U.S. President Harry Truman ordered the dropping of the first atomic bomb on Hiroshima on August 6, 1945. One hundred forty thousand people died right away. Before that, President Roosevelt had said very clearly that in a war you have to try your best to avoid killing innocent people. President Truman had also said the same thing. But the United States had just succeeded in making the first atomic bombs, and the military and political advisors urged him to use them. At that time the Allies were already winning in the Pacific. Yet military and political advisors tried to persuade President Truman to use the atomic bomb. At first he didn't want to do it, because he wanted to avoid taking the life of civilians. But finally they were able to convince him to drop the bomb on the grounds that Japan would surrender after it was dropped, otherwise the war could continue longer and many people would die. If we end the war by killing a number of people now, then we will save the many people who might otherwise have died later. That is the argument, right or wrong. That is a situation where ethics and morality should be applied. It's not easy.

I think the discussion sessions must have been very long before the decision was made to drop the first atomic bomb on Hiroshima. But I know that these discussions did not take into account Right View. President human said that after making this decision he slept like a baby. I low can you sleep well when you know in advance that one hundred forty thousand lives will be taken? Maybe be had spent so many hours listening and discussing that he was exhausted.

The bomb was dropped on the sixth of August, and on

the seventh Japan had not surrendered. On the eighth Japan had still not surrendered. And so there was pressure exerted to drop another bomb. So on August 9, 1945, the second bomb was dropped, this time on Nagasaki, a smaller town. But when the bomb was dropped, seventy thousand people died. And we know that the effects of an atomic bomb are very long-lasting, and many, many people continued to get sick and die from the fallout. This is an extreme example. But a true ethic must be able to deal with these extremes.

THE NOBLE EIGHTFOLD PATH TRANSCENDS ALL OTHER CRITERIA

The Buddha began the Noble Eightfold Path with Right View so that we would have a framework that helps transcend all other criteria in determining right and wrong. Right View is the foundation of all other actions, whether thought, spoken, or acted out. If you've thought through these five sets of criteria and you're still not sure if something is right, you can always return to the base. If we want to look deeply to see if something is right or wrong, we need to use the lens of Right View. Right View is the foundation. Right View is Buddhism's deepest understanding and absolute criterion. In Buddhism we speak of liberation from fear and suffering in terms of understanding. Right View is what liberates us.

RIGHT VIEW

The path leading to well-being has to begin with Right View. Right View is the fruit of our practice of mindfulness and concentration. Instead of beginning the Eightfold Path with Right View, the Buddha could have begun with Right Mindfulness, because mindfulness leads to concentration and concentration leads to insight, or Right View. But Right View is the foundation of all ethical action. When you have Right View, your thinking is Right Thinking, and your speech is Right Speech, and your action is Right Action.

Right View is the view that transcends all views. It is free from discrimination, free from dualistic thinking. As long as you're caught in one view, you can't have Right View. It is possible for us to consider all kinds of views and not to be caught in any of them. When we speak of Right View we don't mean a view that's superior to all other kinds of views. Right View is the absence of all views. We know that all views should be removed. "All views" includes the teachings in this book. All teachings should be considered to be instruments and not absolute truth, even the teachings on impermanence, no-self, and interbeing.

We have to make sure we are focused on insight and not on a particular view. The Buddha used the example of the flame of a match. You have to strike the match skillfully in order to bring about the flame. When the flame has manifested, it will consume the match. When insight is born, it will consume the view. There is no longer any view. You are free. There is insight, not view. It is the insight that liberates you, not the view. This is very important in the teaching of the Buddha. It's like the finger pointing to the moon. If we're not able to look beyond the finger, we can never see the moon.

Attachment to views, intolerance, discrimination, and dogmatism are the foundation for exclusion, fear, anger, craving, and despair. If you are truly practicing Right View, there is no room for these sufferings.

You may be able to remove the notion of permanence. But if in doing so, you get caught in the notion of impermanence, that doesn't help. You have to be free not only from the notion of permanence, but also from the notion of impermanence. You can suffer because you get caught in the notion of self, but you also suffer if you get caught in the notion of nonself. Right View is free from discrimination and dualistic thinking. You don't try to eliminate one thing and retain its opposite. You're not trying to eliminate death and retain only life. You don't have the intention of eliminating nonbeing and retaining only being.

BEING AND NONBEING: THE MANIFESTATION OF A FLAME

Right View is the foundation of well-being, and wrong view is the foundation of ill-being. It's clear that permanence is a wrong view, because according to our observation everything is impermanent, constantly changing; nothing can be the same forever. So immortality is a wrong view. And annihilation—to say that when we die there's nothing left—is also a wrong view. Permanence and annihilation are a pair of opposites. All pairs of opposites are wrong views: being and nonbeing, birth and death, and so on. The notion of being and the notion of nonbeing both create a lot of fear. But with Right View we overcome both notions and we become fearless.

We know that to help the flame to manifest, the match needs to be struck against an object. We know that the flame is partially hidden in the matchbox, and partially hidden outside the matchbox. Outside the matchbox there is oxygen, an essential condition for the manifestation of the flame. Before the flame manifests, should we qualify it as nonexistent? With our practice of looking deeply, we see that everything manifests based on various conditions. When conditions are sufficient, the flame manifests. Once the flame has manifested we tend to say that it exists and is in the realm of being. And we tend to say that before the flame manifested, it belonged to the realm of nonbeing. But reality transcends both notions, being and nonbeing.

NOT THE SAME, NOT DIFFERENT

Suppose I want to light an unlit candle with a lit candle so that I produce another flame. Is this second flame the same flame as the first flame, or is it a totally different flame? That is meditation. When you pick up the family album and look at a picture of yourself when you were five years old, you see that the little boy or girl in the photo is very different from who you are now. Are you the same person as that little girl, or are you a different person? You look so different as far as form is concerned. And you have very different feelings, perceptions, mental formations, and consciousness than you did then. You are quite different from that little girl or little boy. So are you the same person or are you a totally different person? This is an example of another set of notions called sameness and otherness. You're not entirely the same, but you're not totally different.

SUBJECT AND OBJECT

Now we come to a pair of notions that is crucial to our study of Right View: subject and object. We usually believe that our consciousness is the subject of perception; and that there is the world out there, which is the object of our perception; and we think that these two things are completely different. There is consciousness *in* here, the subject of consciousness; and there is the world *out* there, the object of consciousness. According to the Buddha's teaching, that is the basic error.

When you practice mindful breathing, "Breathing in, I'm aware of my in-breath," you practice in such a way that you are no longer an observer. You practice in such a way that you become your in-breath. You become a participant, no longer an outside observer.

In Buddhism, there are six sense organs: eyes, ears, nose, tongue, body, and mind. The first five are physiological and the last is mental. Mind is also an organ, our mental consciousness. The object of the eyes is form. The object of the ears is sound. The object of the nose is smell, of the tongue is taste, and of the body is touch. The object of the mind is dharmas. A dharma is an object of mind, not an objective reality. When we perceive something, that something is the object of our consciousness. The world is just an object of our mind.

Subject and object manifest together at the same time and depend on each other. When you see a mountain, that mountain is the object of your perception, the object of your mind; it's not something separate from your consciousness. To see always means to see *something*. To hear always means to hear something, and so on.

DOUBLE GRASPING

If you believe that there's a subjective consciousness that exists separately from the object of your consciousness, an external world existing separately from your consciousness, then you are caught in an error called double grasping. You are caught by this way of seeing subject and object as two different things. Right View is possible only when you overcome the view that subject and object are two separate entities. We usually think that the left is the opposite of the right. Above is the opposite of below. Being is the opposite of non-being. Life is the opposite of death. Happiness is the opposite of suffering. Sometimes we want just one; we don't want the other. We only want happiness; we don't want suffering.

TAKING TIME TO SEE INTERBEING

To see that subject and object are not separate, we need to train ourselves. Right View takes practice. We have to take our time and live our daily lives in such a way that we can see the nature of interbeing in everything. This requires being more aware in our daily actions. This requires the practice of mindful breathing, mindful sitting, and mindful walking. Only through taking the time to look deeply can we see that happiness and suffering are not individual matters. Our views aren't only something personal. How we view the world affects everything within it.

WE ARE THE PLANET

When we do harm to the environment, we do harm to ourselves; when we do harm to another person, we do harm to ourselves. If we're viewing the world in the light of interbeing and Right View, we can see this right away. The ecosystem and we humans are not two different things. When we kill the ecosystem, we're killing ourselves. We *are* the ecosystem. The ecosystem is us. We are the planet. The planet is us. Anything harmful we do to the environment, we do to ourselves. If the minerals, plants, and animals no longer existed, humans would not exist either. We can only be here if they are here.

WE ARE OUR ANCESTORS

We know very well that we have ancestors. But our ancestors are not only human. We have animal ancestors; we have plant ancestors; and we have mineral ancestors. Our human ancestors are still very young. Human beings appeared very late in the history of life on Earth. Our animal ancestors are still there within us. The reptile, the fish, and the ape are still in our blood. Not only were they part of us in the past, but they continue to exist within us. Just look deeply into our cells. We see that we are the whole history of life.

A SEED OF CORN

If you take one seed of corn and plant it, it will sprout. When it has two leaves, you can ask it if it remembers the time it was a grain of corn. Maybe the cornstalk will be surprised. "Me? A seed of corn? I don't believe it." If so, you could tell it, "Listen, I was there in the very beginning. I brought you home. I put you in this pot. I watered you every day. And I saw you as you sprouted. And from a seed of corn you became a cornstalk. Even if you don't want to accept it, that's the truth."

You could try to convince the cornstalk that it once was a seed of corn, or you could say, "Dear cornstalk, if you look into yourself with intelligence, you can still see the seed of corn alive in you. It no longer has the form of a seed, but it's always in you. You *are* that seed of corn." It may be difficult for the cornstalk to accept. But that is the reality. The stalk is the continuation of the seed.

You can approach a young person and tell him, "You are the continuation of your father. You *are* your father, because your father is fully present in every cell of your body." That is the truth. Whatever you do, your father is doing that with you. When you are angry, your father gets angry. When you get angry with yourself, you get angry with your father. And when you get angry with your father, you get angry with yourself. Especially if the young person has a difficult relationship with his father, or if he didn't know his father, these things may be hard to accept. But that is the truth.

With mindfulness and concentration, you naturally begin to see things more deeply. You can tell that your body is not just yours. It's also the body of your parents, your ancestors, and all the living species that came before you. If you look deeply in this way, you see that your cells will also live on in all your descendants. All those who come after you will be part of your continuation. You can see that you are the continuation of your parents with all their positive qualities, talents, and beauty. But you can also see all their difficulties, and challenges living within you. You can transform their suffering for their benefit as well as your own.

GREAT TOGETHERNESS: NO COMPLEXES

When you have Right View and are able to see your ancestors and descendants in you, then you can have a great togetherness. This very body contains so many elements: our ancestors and descendants, what we consume, the earth, the sun, and the whole cosmos. Our practice is to live harmoniously with all these elements, which are both within us and around us. The view that we have a separate self is like a prison. When you are imprisoned in your wrong views, you suffer from comparing yourself to others both inside and outside of your family. We may feel hurt by others, or we may feel proud that we are different and separate from them. "Oh, I have nothing to do with that woman, my mother; she's so difficult for me. I have nothing to do with my father who always verbally abused me and even beat me; I have nothing to do with that man." But the seeds of our ancestors are in us. Breathing in, I see that my father is still in every one of my cells. My mother is in every cell. When you are aware of nonself, there is no question of being greater than, less than, or equal to anybody else, because you and that other person are not separate.

If we're not mindful, we only perceive a few parts of ourselves. We pick and choose based on our experience and decide that we are this or that kind of person. Practicing meditation is to recognize your whole self, with all these parts you've received from your ancestors, both their strengths and weaknesses. This may feel intellectual. But if you practice mindful awareness and meditation, you will begin to recognize it. Practicing meditation is practicing Right View. You will see deeply that you are the child, the sibling, and the parent. You are the person you hate and the person you love. You need to experience this for yourself to believe it.

SEEING WITH OUR ANCESTORS' EYES

One day I looked outside at the mountain, and I saw so clearly that as I was looking at these mountains, all my ancestors—my father, my mother, my grandparents, all the lineages of human ancestors—were in me and were looking at the mountain together with me. We saw the beautiful dawn together and enjoyed a concert of color.

My eyes belong to me and also to my ancestors. All those ancestors were admiring the wonderful rising sun with me. For many generations, my ancestors worked hard and had many worries and many moments of stress, anger, and fear. Maybe they never had a chance to sit quietly, peacefully, happily, to be with that great togetherness. They never had a chance to sit quietly and follow their breath, to be centered and to be in touch with their wonderful environment. So when we stop like that, all our ancestors stop at the same time, well synchronized, because they are in our body, in every one of our cells. Now *we* have a chance to stop. If we are able to stop, we stop for them all, and all of them are stopping together with us.

The moment when we can stop, and we can be in touch with that majestic dawn, that is an awakened moment. You are not enlightened as an individual self. Enlightenment is the moment you are in touch deeply with all your ancestors and descendants and are sharing with them your peace, your joy, and your happiness. That doesn't mean stopping all sense of oneself. But you can smile, and know that all of them are smiling your wonderful smile. You walk peacefully, and all of them are walking peacefully with you.

WE ARE EACH OTHER

We need to see the interconnection between ourselves and others. Palestinians and Israelis need to see the interconnection with each other, to see that they are one. Although Christians, Muslims, and Jews come from one root, they behave like the cornstalk who forgets that she was born from the seed of corn.

RIGHT THINKING (NONDISCRIMINATION)

The Noble Eightfold Path offered by the Buddha does not begin with Right Thinking, because Right Thinking must be based on

Right View. Right View gives us the deep understanding that leads to Right Thinking. Right Thinking has the connotation of right intention in it. When you think, you also express your intention. In the creation of the code of ethics based on the insight of Right View, our intention is the starting point.

Right Thinking is thinking that embodies the insight of nonduality, emptiness, and interbeing. It is possible for us to produce thoughts that go along with this kind of insight. Such thoughts will heal us and heal the world, because they remove separation and despair.

Right Thinking is the thinking that goes along with understanding and compassion. If we produce a thought that doesn't have understanding and compassion, it's not Right. Thinking. Right Thinking brings well-being. As soon as we produce a thought of reconciliation, compassion, understanding, and nondiscrimination, we feel healing taking place in our bodies and minds, and we feel better right away. Right Thinking can heal and transform.

If we produce a thought in line with wrong thinking, a thought that's full of hate, anger, or despair, it destroys our health, our harmony, and makes us suffer. It brings ill-being to us right away, and it also brings ill-being to the world.

Right Thinking is thinking that goes in the direction of nondiscrimination, the kind of thinking that goes in the direction of understanding and compassion. We can always produce a thought that's free from discrimination, free from dualistic thinking, free from anger and separation, and full of understanding and compassion. If discrimination is still there, love and understanding are not possible.

There is a wisdom called the Wisdom of Nondiscrimination. When we're able to produce a thought in line with Right

Thinking, full of compassion and understanding, that thought immediately begins to heal us and heal the world. When we produce a thought of division, hatred, and anger, that thought begins to destroy our body and mind and begins to destroy the world. It's a destructive thought.

If we look into our body, we see that birth and death occur every second. Millions of cells are dying and new ones are being born inside us at each moment. Birth and death lean on each other to be possible. With that insight, we're no longer afraid of dying. Birth, life, and death, always co-exist in the present moment. You don't need to wait until the moment you die in order to make peace with death. If death is there, life is also there, because death and life are interconnected.

We have been used to thinking dualistically, and we suffer because of that. That's why we have to train ourselves in nondualistic thinking, thinking that's informed by Right View. It's very easy for us to produce a thought in line with nondiscrimination, understanding, and love, a thought that has the power to heal ourselves and heal the world. Your thoughts are your continuation. In Buddhism, thinking is already action. By your thinking, you can destroy the world. But it's equally true that your thinking can save the world and bring healing.

YOUR THOUGHT BEARS YOUR SIGNATURE

When you produce a thought, it bears your signature. It's you who has produced that thought. You are responsible for it. If it's a thought of compassion, forgiveness, or nondiscrimination, you will continue beautifully into the future, because that thought has your signature in it. You are the author of the action. This is also true about what you say. If what you say expresses forgiveness, compassion, or nondiscrimination, your words bear your signature. You can't say, "No, I didn't say that." You *did* say that. Your signature is in it; you can't deny that. Action is the same. Whatever you have done bears your signature. Even when your body is no longer there, your thought continues.

RIGHT SPEECH

Right Speech is the third element of the Noble Eightfold Path. Whenever you say or write something—whether professionally or personally—it should be said with awareness of nondiscrimination, understanding, and compassion. What you say can heal yourself, others, and the world. We know that much suffering is caused by wrong speech.

There are four guidelines concerning Right Speech, 1. Speak truthfully, without lies. 2. Speak consistently, without saying one thing to one person and something else to another. 3. Speak respectfully, without insult. 4. Speak accurately, without exaggeration. Then we are practicing Right Speech.

When you have Right Thinking you know how to have Right Speech. You know that your beloved is impermanent; his mind is impermanent; and his body is impermanent. Yet in daily life you presume that he is permanent, and so you take him for granted. Right Thinking means you know he is impermanent. With this insight, you won't be angry; you'll try to do and say things in a different way. So don't speak harshly, saying, "He betrayed me." Instead say, "Oh, I see that I'm partly to blame for the situation," or "I'm responsible for not handling that situation well," and so on. Then you have Right Speech.

Imagine you're sitting down to write a letter full of forgiveness and compassion. While you're writing that letter, you're healing yourself. Even if the other person hasn't yet read your letter, the world around you begins to heal. You can practice Right Speech when you send an email, and it can relieve the suffering inside you and the suffering in the other person right away. Why wait? We can always practice Right Speech to heal ourselves, to reconcile with ourselves and with the world.

Right Speech is speech that expresses nondiscrimination, forgiveness, understanding, support, and love. We know that when we're able to say or write something like that, we feel wonderful. It's so liberating and healing; it brings relief. Right Speech brings well-being. Anything that we say that contains discrimination, hate, and the desire to punish will make us suffer and will make others suffer.

SPEAK SKILLFULLY SO THE TEACHINGS AREN'T MISUNDERSTOOD

When the Buddha spoke about emptiness, *shunyata,* he was very afraid that his students would take it as a view. When he spoke about no-self, he was afraid that his students would take this as a view as well. We're generally caught in the view of self. We can also be caught in the view of no-self. When our foundation is Right View, the emptiness of all views, we are free from the view of self and no-self. When you speak, you must be careful to use words and images that are informed by Right View. Speak skillfully, and whatever you offer, offer it skillfully, so that the other person won't get caught in a view. The Buddha said, "My teaching is like a finger pointing to the moon. It's not my intention to show you my finger. It's my intention to show you the moon in the sky. But if you take my finger to be the moon, you will be lost."

OBAMA'S EGYPT SPEECH

In the speech President Obama gave at Cairo University on June 4, 2009, he used Right Speech in his attempt to ease tension between the United States and the Islamic world. He talked with humility, recognizing the values of Islam and Islamic people. That kind of loving speech belongs to the Eightfold Noble Path; it can release the tension in international affairs. Obama said: "I want to begin anew with Islam." The U.S. and Muslims are not enemies. The U.S. should not exclude Muslims, and Muslims should not exclude the U.S. We recognize all the good things that Islam has offered to the heritage and culture of humankind. Obama is one of the few politicians who knows how to use loving speech, with humility. A speech alone, if it is Right Speech, could help remove a lot of suffering.

Much suffering is brought about by wrong speech. Wrong speech is speech that does not have openness, that does not have understanding, compassion, and reconciliation. When we write something, when we say something on the telephone, what we say should be Right Speech. It should convey our insight, understanding, and compassion. When we practice Right Speech, we feel wonderful in our body and our mind. And the one who listens to us feels wonderful also. It's possible for us to use Right Speech, the speech of compassion, tolerance, and forgiveness several times a day. It doesn't cost anything. And it heals. It heals us and it heals the world.

RIGHT ACTION

The Sanskrit word *karma* means action. The meaning also includes the results of our actions. Action in Buddhism is threefold—action of body, speech, and mind. Thinking is already action; speech is action; and bodily movement is action. What you produce in terms of thought, speech, and action is your continuation, your karma. The dissolution of this body does not affect your continuation. In every moment we are producing the three kinds of action: thought, speech, and physical action. Our actions will have an effect on us and on the world. Your karma can assure a beautiful and a better continuation. If we know how to handle our thinking, speech, and action, we will continue to create happiness in the world, even when our body is no longer present in its current form.

Thinking is the first kind of action. Thinking can affect the world. If you think wrongly, the world will suffer, and you will suffer as well. So you have to practice Right Thinking. Thoughts in line with Right Thinking express elements of nondiscrimination, interbeing, understanding, forgiveness, and compassion. Such a thought will have an effect right away on you, your health, your mind, and on the world. By producing Right Thinking you can heal yourself, your body, and your mind. If your thinking is wrong, it destroys your body and your mind. It's very important to learn how to produce a thought of compassion, forgiveness, understanding, and nondiscrimination. Right Thinking can heal you and heal the world.

Speaking can also change the world. If we're capable of saying or writing something in line with compassion, understanding, nondiscrimination, and inclusiveness, we feel wonderful in our body and in our mind. That kind of speech will have a healing effect. After you've been able to say something kind, forgiving, and compassionate, you feel much better. When you write a letter full of compassion and forgiveness, you feel very good within yourself. Although the other person hasn't yet read it, you haven't yet posted the letter, you feel wonderful and liberated already. Right Speech can heal, can liberate—it can heal and liberate you, and help to heal and liberate other people in the world. Speech is the second form of action.

The third form of action is bodily action. If you do something that supports, protects, comforts, or saves someone, you feel wonderful within yourself. You get the effect right away. Triple action involves body, speech, and mind.

With the insight of interbeing, no self, and nonduality, our thinking will have a chance to be Right Thinking, our words will have a chance to be Right Speech, and our action will have a chance to be Right Action. Every thought, every word, every act of ours bears our signature. Our karma continues us. Our notions of permanence and annihilation should be transcended in order for us to have Right View. Right View is the absence of all views, including the views of permanence and annihilation.

So if we have lost someone who is very close to us, and we are grieving her death, we have to look again. That person is still continuing. We can do something to help her to continue more beautifully. She is still alive inside us and around us. With our new way of looking, we can still recognize her all around, the same way we recognize our cloud in the cup of tea.

When you drink your cup of tea with mindfulness and concentration you can have the insight that the cloud is in your tea, very close. You have never lost her. She is still alive, very near you. She may be in a new form, different than in the past. That is the kind of insight we should have to overcome grief. We think that we have lost her. But she hasn't died; she hasn't disappeared. She continues in her new form. And we have to practice looking deeply in order to recognize her continuation, and support that. By producing Right Thinking, Right Speech, and Right Action, we can support her. "Darling, I know you are there somehow, very real to me. I am breathing for you. I am looking around for you. I enjoy life for you. And I know that you are still there very close to me and you are in me." In this way, we can transform our suffering and feel much better.

If you have the insight of interbeing, what you think will be Right Thinking; what you say will be Right Speech; and what you do will be Right Action. It will be very easy for you to select the kind of livelihood that can express compassion and understanding. You know how to make good use of your time to transform suffering into happiness and help people.

Karma is like a savings account where you deposit your thought, speech, and action. Your action continues always, even after the dissolution of this body. The thinking, the speaking, and the acting is what we perform every day.

We can offer our thinking, our speech, and our actions to the world. That is our individual contribution to global healing and to a global ethic. It is possible to offer the best kind of thinking, the best kind of speech, and the best kind of action; those are our products, our continuation. They will not be lost. They will continue in the cosmos. The effects of our thinking, speech, and action will continue whether this body is still here or has disintegrated.

The Buddha wants us to pay attention to each of the three kinds of action, so each is a category of the Noble Eightfold Path. Right Action refers particularly to right bodily action. Thinking and speaking are listed separately. Right bodily action brings relief, support, protection, and saves the lives of people, animals, plants, and minerals. Right Action can help protect the environment and reverse the process of global climate change. Right Action is possible in the here and the now. Consuming in mindfulness is also Right Action. Right Action brings well-being just as wrong action brings ill-being.

RIGHT LIVELIHOOD

Right Livelihood is the kind of occupation that will not make us suffer, and by which we can express our ideal of compassion and understanding. Those of us who have the kind of job that can help us express our love, our care, and our compassion should be happy about that. It's wonderful to have that kind of livelihood. Even if it brings less money, it brings much happiness. You know you're on the right path, and that alone can make you happy. Right Livelihood brings well-being. Wrong livelihood brings ill-being. It destroys our planet and creates toxins that enter our bodies and minds. The Noble Eightfold Path recommends Right Livelihood. We know that the cause of suffering lies in wrong livelihood, when we earn our living in a way that does damage to ourselves and others.

Suppose our nation is selling weapons to poor countries, and it's become a very important industry of the nation. Many industrialized countries sell weapons to poorer countries. That is not Right Livelihood. Imagine a little boy holding an empty plate for many hours without receiving anything to eat, but someone offers him grenades and bombs and guns. It doesn't make sense.

If you're a filmmaker, you know that violent films sell very well. But when people consume these films, they consume a lot of violence, anger, and fear. People get intoxicated by these films every day. Or perhaps you make cars that consume a lot of gasoline, simply because people want to buy them. You're not thinking about the pollution or the shortage of energy. When we practice Right Livelihood, we think about the impact of our work, not just its profitability.

RIGHT DILIGENCE

The term *samyak pradbana* is sometimes translated as Right Effort. I prefer the word "diligence" to the word "effort," because an effort can make you tired. But when you're diligent, you don't need to be tired. Don't practice mindfulness intensively. Just practice regularly and diligently. There are those of us who practice very intensively for a few weeks, and then after that we abandon the practice. There are those of us who practice regularly, not intensively, but continuously.

If someone asks you why you practice meditation or mindful awareness, a good answer might be, "Because I like it" or "Because I enjoy doing it." If you don't enjoy the practice, you have to make an effort. In making an effort you get tired, and finally you abandon the practice.

The best reason to do some element of the practice is, "Because I like it." Why do you practice walking meditation? Because I like it. Why do you eat vegetarian food? Because I like it. If you like it, you will continue to do it. Right Diligence brings well-being. The practice of mindful walking and movement, and the practice of mindful breathing and smiling bring well-being, peace, and happiness. After enlightenment the Buddha continued to practice. The Buddha was already a Buddha, so why did he have to practice walking mindfully? Because he liked it.

WRONG DILIGENCE

There are those of us who are very diligent, but our diligence is wrong diligence. Wrong diligence can bring ill-being. We are caught in our work, for example, and we don't take care of ourselves or our loved ones. They are caught, sucked into the work. We can work very hard and make a lot of effort but still have no happiness. Many of us are running around too much and are stressed from the practice of wrong diligence. Instead of practicing diligence to go in the direction of insight, we are diligently going in search of money, fame, or pleasure.

FOUR TOOLS FOR RIGHT DILIGENCE

The Buddha described Right Diligence in four steps. The four steps involve practicing mindfulness in such a way that we focus on watering the positive seeds within us and giving the negative seeds a rest. The four steps inter-are; each step contains the other three. In Buddhist psychology, our consciousness is represented by a circle with two layers. The lower level of our consciousness is called store consciousness, and it contains all the seeds of well-being and ill-being. When we water a seed with our awareness, it becomes energized and comes up to the upper level called mind consciousness. Once in mind consciousness, it's no longer called a seed, but a mental formation. Mind consciousness is like the living room, and store consciousness is like the basement. Usually we put in the basement the things we don't like or don't want in our living room.

The first step in Right Diligence is to try our best to not allow the unbeneficial seeds to manifest. In us there are beneficial and unbeneficial seeds. In the depths of our consciousness there are seeds of love, compassion, joy, forgiveness, and so on. All these very beneficial things are in us. It's like the many kinds of bacteria in our intestines or in our mouth; there are beneficial microflora that are very useful. But there are also other seeds in store consciousness—our anger, fear, despair, and trauma are all there.

The first step of Right Diligence is to be attentive and skillful enough not to allow the unbeneficial seeds to manifest. We allow them to sleep quietly and peacefully down there in store consciousness. Don't go down and set them off, because when we wake them up, they may cause trouble.

The second aspect of practice is that if by chance the seed of anger, despair, jealousy, suffering, or trauma has already manifested as a mental formation, we *do* something in order to help it to go back down to sleep again as a seed in store consciousness. When a seed manifests in mind consciousness and stays there for a long time, the seed grows stronger at the base. So if an unbeneficial mental formation manifests, don't allow it to stay too long. Do something to help it go back—not suppressing it, but helping it to go back. One way is to invite a beneficial seed to come up and replace it.

CHANGING THE PEG

The Buddha uses the image of a carpenter's peg. To join two pieces of wood, the carpenter makes a hole in each, aligns the holes, and drives in a peg. But if a peg becomes rotten or is no longer good, he changes the peg by using a new peg to drive the old one out and replace it. Changing the peg is a recommendation made by the Buddha. When an unbeneficial mental formation manifests, the practitioner should know how to replace it with a good one. We can use the image of a CD. If a CD doesn't please us, why do we have to keep listening to it? We can change the CD. If we don't like anger or despair, why do we have to sit there and suffer? If we don't want to keep watching a particular film or tv program, we can change the channel. There are positive seeds in us of compassion, love, joy, and peace. So invite them up. It's very pleasant, and it can change the situation right away. You don't have to fight or suppress the other mental formation.

The third aspect of Right Diligence is to invite the beneficial seeds to come up. Think of a beneficial seed as you would a friend you haven't seen for a while. Her presence in the living room brings a lot of joy. So send her an invitation. You know that her presence in your living room will dissipate the darkness and sorrow. That friend is in you—the capacity to be happy, joyful, and compassionate—and these friends are always available. We should invite them into the living room often. It's not too difficult to do. Every time I have a friend like that in my living room, I enjoy it very much. Joy and happiness are always possible. We can create a feeling of joy, happiness, serenity, peace, self-fulfillment, or forgiveness by giving the beneficial things a chance to manifest.

The fourth aspect of the practice of Right Diligence is that when something beneficial arises, we try to keep it with us as long as possible in the living room, like a friend. When a good friend has come to your living room, you want her to stay. The longer a beneficial seed stays in the living room, the stronger it will become. When good things arise, try to keep them in mind consciousness. At the base that good seed will continue to grow, and the next time it will manifest more easily. Sometimes you don't have to invite that seed up, it just comes into your living room. Happiness becomes a regular thing, a normal thing. Before, happiness was not normal; we would only be happy from time to time. But if the seeds of happiness and love have become strong, they will manifest by themselves without invitation and we will welcome them.

These four practices of Right Diligence take practice. Keep the difficult seeds sleeping down there; don't invite them up. But if they have manifested, try your best to let them go back down to store consciousness as soon as possible. As for the good things that haven't manifested, invite them to manifest. And when they have manifested, invite them to stay longer. That is the true meaning of diligence. It can bring so much happiness.

RIGHT MINDFULNESS

The path of the Buddha can be understood in terms of energy. We know that mindfulness is an energy that we generate during our practice; generating mindfulness is the basic practice. Mindfulness is the kind of energy that helps us to be *here,* established in the present moment. Mindfulness helps bring the mind back to the body, so we can be truly present, truly alive, and able to touch the wonders of life that are available to us right now. Mindfulness helps us to be aware of what is going on inside us—our happiness and also our suffering. Mindfulness helps us handle our happiness and our suffering, as well as to handle the suffering of the world and to work for the happiness of the world.

The energy of mindfulness carries with it the energy of concentration. When you're mindful of something, you're somehow already concentrated on that thing When you bring your attention to something, if you can preserve and keep your mindfulness alive, you'll naturally be concentrated on the object of your mind. The more concentrated you are, the more mindful you become. So the two energies support each other.

When your mindfulness and concentration are powerful enough, you begin to have insight. Insight is enlightenment, is understanding. We don't have to practice for a certain number of years in order to have insight. Insight can be our daily business. Whenever there is mindfulness, there is already some insight.

Suppose you're breathing in mindfully. This is already insight, because although everyone is breathing, not everyone is aware that they are breathing. You're aware that you're breathing in. That's already insight; that's already enlightenment; that's already awakening. When you breathe in mindfully, you can realize that you are alive—because if you were not alive, you would not be breathing in. So breathing in, you gain the insight that you are alive. And to be alive is something very important. It's a miracle, the greatest of all miracles, and you can rejoice in life. You can breathe in such a way that your in-breath is a kind of celebration. With your in-breath you celebrate being alive.

The practice of mindful breathing can be very deep, because it brings mindfulness, concentration, and insight. When we have insight we know what to do and what not to do; what to say and what not to say; what to think and what not to think. The three kinds of energy you generate in your practice are the foundation of any kind of ethics. You can't speak about morality, ethics, or a code of behavior without speaking of mindfulness, concentration, and insight. It is with the energy of mindfulness, concentration, and insight that you can find a path, build a path, and offer a path for humanity—a path that will lead to peace and happiness, a path of transformation and healing. It's so important that whenever we reflect on the subject of a global ethic, we always do so in terms of the practice. Our basic practice is the practice of generating the energy of mindfulness, concentration, and insight. Insight will bring compassion, love, harmony, and peace.

When we practice Right Mindfulness, we bring about Right Concentration. With Right Concentration, we can overcome all wrong views and arrive at the insight that liberates us from fear, despair, and anger. Insight is possible only with the energy of mindfulness and concentration.

Mindfulness is the kind of energy that brings our minds back to our bodies so that we can be well established in the present moment, and truly live our lives. Mindfulness allows us to be aware of what is going on in the present moment—in our bodies, in our feelings, in our perceptions, and in the world. So how can there be wrong mindfulness? Why do we need to talk of Right Mindfulness?

If we keep thinking of the things that bring us sorrow and fear, or if we're full of worries about the future, we have no space for Right Mindfulness. It's a natural tendency to focus our mindfulness on the past, because we have lived, and every experience of our lives is stored in store consciousness. In our daily lives, we're used to sliding back to the past. The little child in us is used to that environment. The child doesn't want to come out with us into the present moment. It's become a habit to listen to that child call you back to the past. You find it more comfortable to be in the past. But we know that your life is here and now. We are no longer as fragile or vulnerable as when we were children. We are very capable of living safely in the present moment.

You can always come home to the present moment. You may have the habit of visiting the past, and you think that the past is your home. You always want to go home. You feel comfortable there—you're comfortable, but you suffer. We say, "There's no place like home." But the past is not your true home. Your true home is in the here and the now. Only in the here and the now can you encounter real life. In the past you can encounter only memories.

There is still a lot of fear, anxiety, and anguish in us. Wrong diligence, focusing tirelessly on the past or on the future, leads to wrong mindfulness. If we are only focused on how to obtain power, money, or guaranteed safety, this is wrong mindfulness. We are driven by our cravings and completely forget to see that life around us is so beautiful. With Right Mindfulness, we dwell in the present moment, in touch with what is still positive inside and around us.

BREATHING YOUR WAY HOME

When we get pulled away from Right Mindfulness, bringing our body and mind back together can bring us home to the present moment. Usually it is our mind that leaves and goes into the past or the future while our body stays right here. But with mindfulness we can always come back to our body.

When we recognize the presence of tension in us and we can release it, our mindfulness grows stronger. If we see the presence of our suffering and its causes, we know we don't want that suffering any longer. Just acknowledging that we don't want to have that tension or that suffering inside us puts us in touch with the Third Noble Truth, well-being. When you eliminate the causes of tension, you are more relaxed, and you have more happiness. The way to release all these tensions is with our mindful breath. So we always start with mindfulness.

Mindfulness brings the mind to the present moment, and we see and experience things more deeply.

Going back to the present moment you can see if your body is tense. We look deeply and see that, "Ah, I am tense because I'm carried away by my worry, anxiety, and plans." Then we can make the determination not to be carried away like that. When you have Right Mindfulness, you see deeply what brings you suffering and what brings you happiness. Right Mindfulness is the awareness that you can be relaxed, happy, and at peace right away. Then you no longer feel the need to run away.

RIGHT CONCENTRATION

Right Mindfulness carries Right Concentration. When you have concentration you' see things more deeply and have more insight. Mindfulness brings concentration, which in turn brings you insight about how to behave more ethically. Right Mindfulness and Right Concentration help us look deeply into the nature of reality and arrive at the insights of nondiscrimination and interbeing. The best thing we can offer to the world is our insight. To live our life in mindfulness and with concentration is to continue to produce insight—for our own liberation, healing, and nourishment, and for the liberation, healing, and nourishment of the world.

CONCENTRATE ON SOMETHING INTERESTING

Concentration is always concentration on something, and it's very easy to concentrate if the object of your concentration is interesting. You don't need to go to a retreat or sit in meditation in order to do that. You can do it at any time. Anything can be interesting. For a scientist, a piece of dust is very interesting; there's a lot to explore in a piece of dust. For a biologist, a leaf can be intriguing. We need to find objects of concentration that interest us.

CONCENTRATION ON IMPERMANENCE

Impermanence is an important object of our concentration. Things are impermanent. Even if a person is hurtful, thanks to impermanence that person may encounter some good conditions that allow him to become a less angry person. Our situation may be bad, but thanks to our awareness of impermanence we can cultivate a more positive view, and perhaps the situation can improve. That is the fruit of Right Concentration.

Wrong concentration only brings us suffering. Suppose someone concentrates on obtaining the object of his craving. If the object of his concentration is power, money, fame, sex, or infatuation, his mind will tend to be carried away by that and he will make himself and others suffer greatly.

MANY CONCENTRATIONS

Some people have misperceptions about Buddhism and they think it's very pessimistic. Buddhist teachings say that everything is empty. Some people misperceive this and think of emptiness as negative. It is true that Buddhism says we are empty of a separate self. But we are full of the whole universe.

In Buddhism we have many doors to insight, many concentrations and practices for looking deeply. There are people who only look into impermanence and they perceive how all things change. They only use the door of impermanence, hut for them that may well be the door that can open to enlightenment. There are those who look at emptiness; they can be enlightened too. There are those who look at the door of dependent co-arising and they see that many conditions are required for something to manifest. They see a flame and know that not only the match, but the oxygen, the matchbox, and the person who strikes the match must all come together for that flame to manifest.

Looking deeply into one door, you see all the other doors. The insight that there are many paths to enlightenment is the fruit of our practice and is the ground of morality and ethics. There are many different concentrations we can practice, but our concentration must be Right Concentration. Without Right Mindfulness and Right Concentration, there is no way to arrive at insight.

THE NOBLE EIGHTFOLD PATH AS THE WAY OUT OF PAIN

When we look deeply into the nature of ill-being, we see so much tension, pain, and suffering. We hold our suffering in our bodies, in our relationships, in our emotions, and this influences how we think and act in the world. We ask what Buddhism can do to release that tension, pain, and suffering. The answer is that it can remind us that this suffering eases when we follow the Eightfold Path.

The path of the eight right practices is a path for everyone, not just for monks and nuns or for Buddhists, but for everyone living in the world. We have to live our daily lives in such a way that we live deeply in mindfulness, so that we can see the nature of interbeing in everything. Following the Noble Eightfold Path brings us joy and ease and helps transform intolerance, dogmatism, attachment to views, discrimination, and violence.

7

WALKING THE NOBLE EIGHTFOLD PATH

THE FIVE MINDFULNESS TRAININGS

The Five Mindfulness Trainings represent the Buddhist vision for a global spirituality and a global ethic. They are a concrete expression of the Buddha's teachings on the Four Noble Truths and the Noble Eightfold Path, the path of right understanding and true love, which leads to healing, transformation, and happiness for ourselves and for the world. To practice the Five Mindfulness Trainings is to cultivate the insight of interbeing. This is Right View, which can remove all discrimination, intolerance, anger, fear, and despair. If we live according to the Five Mindfulness Trainings, we are already on the path of a bodhisattva. Knowing we are on that path, we are not lost in confusion about our life in the present, in preoccupation with the past, or in fears about the future.

When we practice the mindfulness trainings, we make a commitment to refrain from behaviors that harm ourselves and others. We commit to not killing, not stealing, not engaging in sexual misconduct, not speaking falsely, and to abstaining from intoxicants. The first training is to protect life, to decrease violence in oneself, in the family, and in society. The second training is to practice social justice, generosity, not stealing, and not exploiting other living beings. The third training is the practice of responsible sexual behavior in order to protect individuals, couples, families, and children. The fourth training is the practice of deep listening and loving speech in order to restore communication and bring reconciliation. The fifth training is to practice mindful consumption, not bringing toxins into our bodies and minds, not consuming tv programs, magazines, films, and so on that may contain poisons such as violence, craving, and hatred. The practice of mindful consumption is the practice of protecting ourselves, our families, our society, and our communities.

These trainings have come from our understanding of the Noble Eightfold Path. For example, the root of suffering is not only that people kill. The killing happens because we have a wrong perception, a wrong view. If we have wrong views, we may be ready to kill. But if we see clearly and have Right View, we have neither the ability nor the desire to kill. With Right View, we see clearly that whatever we want to kill is part of us; it is like our own family member, and we lose our ability to harm it.

The Five Mindfulness Trainings are offered without dogma or religion. Everybody can use them as an ethics for their life without becoming Buddhist or becoming part of any tradition or faith. You are just yourself, but you try to make a beautiful life by following these guidelines.

The Five Mindfulness Trainings are not commandments; they don't come from an external god. They come from our own wisdom and insight. The insight they contain is the outcome of our practice of mindfulness and concentration.

The trainings can be a joy, not something we *have* to do. It's like when we refrain from polluting the planet or we refrain from eating too much meat, we don't feel that we're suffering because of it. In fact we feel that we're very lucky to be able to consume and to live in such a way that makes a future for the planet a real possibility. If, with your practice of the Five Mindfulness Trainings, you feel that your understanding, loving kindness, and compassion have increased, then you can share your practice with others and in that way we can make the world better.

THE FIVE MINDFULNESS TRAININGS

1. Reverence for Life

Aware of the suffering caused by the destruction of life, I am committed to cultivating the insight of interbeing and compassion and learning ways to protect the lives of people, animals, plants, and minerals. I am determined not to kill, not to let others kill, and not to support any act of killing in the world, in my thinking, or in my way of life. Seeing that harmful actions arise from anger, fear, greed, and intolerance, which in turn come from dualistic and discriminative thinking, I will cultivate openness, nondiscrimination, and nonattachment to views in order to transform violence, fanaticism, and dogmatism in myself and in the world.

2. True Happiness

Aware of the suffering caused by exploitation, social injustice, stealing, and oppression, I am committed to practicing generosity in my thinking, speaking, and acting. I am determined not to steal and not to possess anything that should belong to others; and I will share my time, energy, and material resources with those who are in need. I will practice looking deeply to see that the happiness and suffering of others are not separate from my own happiness and suffering; that true happiness is not possible without understanding and compassion; and that running after wealth, fame, power, and sensual pleasures can bring much suffering and despair. I am aware that happiness depends on my mental attitude and not on external conditions, and that I can live happily in the present moment simply by remembering that I already have more than enough conditions to be happy. I am committed to practicing Right Livelihood so that I can help reduce the suffering of living beings on Earth and reverse the process of global warming.

3. True Love

Aware of the suffering caused by sexual misconduct, I am committed to cultivating responsibility and learning ways to protect the safety and integrity of individuals, couples, families, and society. Knowing that sexual desire is not love, and that sexual activity motivated by craving always harms myself as well as others, I am determined not to engage in sexual relations without true love and a deep, long-term commitment made known to my family and friends. I will do everything in my power to protect children from sexual abuse and to prevent couples and families from being broken by sexual misconduct. Seeing that body and mind are one, I am committed to learning appropriate ways to take care of my sexual energy and cultivating loving kindness, compassion, joy, and inclusiveness—which are the four basic elements of true love—for my greater happiness and the greater happiness of others. Practicing true love, we know that we will continue beautifully into the future.

4. Loving Speech and Deep Listening

Aware of the suffering caused by unmindful speech and the

inability to listen to others, I am committed to cultivating loving speech and compassionate listening in order to relieve suffering and to promote reconciliation and peace in myself and among other people, ethnic and religious groups, and nations. Knowing that words can create happiness or suffering, I am committed to speaking truthfully using words that inspire confidence, joy, and hope. When anger is manifesting in me, I am determined not to speak. I will practice mindful breathing in order to recognize and to look deeply into my anger. I know that the roots of anger can be found in my wrong perceptions and lack of understanding of the suffering in myself and in the other person. I will speak and listen in a way that can help myself and the other person to transform suffering and see the way out of difficult situations. I am determined not to spread news that I do not know to be certain and not to utter words that can cause division or discord.

I will practice Right Diligence to nourish my capacity for understanding, love, joy, and inclusiveness, and gradually transform anger, violence, and fear that lie deep in my consciousness.

5. Nourishment and Healing

Aware of the suffering caused by unmindful consumption, I am committed to cultivating good health, both physical and mental, for myself, my family, and my society by practicing mindful eating, drinking, and consuming. I will practice looking deeply into how I consume the Four Kinds of Nutriments, namely edible foods, sense impressions, volition, and consciousness. I am determined not to gamble, or to use alcohol, drugs, or any other products that contain toxins, such as certain websites, electronic games, TV programs, films, magazines, books, and conversations.

I will practice coming back to the present moment to be in touch with the refreshing, healing, and nourishing elements in me and around me, not letting regrets and sorrow drag me back into the past nor letting anxieties, fear, or craving pull me out of the present moment. I am determined not to try to cover up loneliness, anxiety, or other suffering by losing myself in consumption. I will contemplate interbeing and consume in a way that preserves peace, joy, and well-being in my body and consciousness, and in the collective body and consciousness of my family, my society, and the Earth.

THE FIVE MINDFULNESS TRAININGS COME FROM OUR PRACTICE

When we study and practice the Five Mindfulness Trainings, we are aware that the five trainings are the fruit of our meditation. They are born from our mindfulness and concentration. They represent our insight. We need to practice them daily with a lot of openness and joy.

We know that killing has been going on in many places in the world due to fanaticism, narrow-mindedness, and wrong thinking. If we just say that killing is not good, that is not very helpful. But if we know how to help the person who has the desire to kill, and we can help him get the insight of interbeing, remove fanaticism and narrowness, then naturally that person will not have that same desire to harm anymore.

INTERBEING AND THE FIRST MINDFULNESS TRAINING

People are killing each other, and it's because they don't have the insight of interbeing. They don't see that the person they're killing is themselves. If we just advise people not to kill, that may not be enough. We have to inspire them. We have to help them to understand that killing someone is killing yourself. If you're inhabited by the insight of interbeing, you *know* that killing someone is killing yourself. The first mindfulness training, not to kill, always to protect life, should not be just a commandment, someone telling you that it's a good thing to do. But you have to understand *why* you should not kill. If you can touch the insight of interbeing, and you are free from double grasping—the illusion that subject and object are separate from each other—then you see very clearly that killing the other is to kill yourself.

A person who is free from all views, a person who is capable of seeing the interbeing nature of everything, will never have the desire to kill. The practice of the First Mindfulness Training nourishes our compassion. Compassion benefits us and makes us happy. Without compassion we cannot relate to the world and to other living beings; communication is impossible. That's why cultivating compassion is crucial. It will bring well-being to us and to the world. It is a training; we need to train ourselves to be able to help compassion grow day by day.

There were moments during the Vietnam War when we were very close to despair. The war was dragging on and we did not see any sign that it would end. Every day, every night, people died, and the country was being destroyed by bombs and chemicals. The young people came to me and asked, "Thay, is there any hope that the war will end soon?"

At that moment, we did not see any hope. We were very close to despair, because the war went on and on for a long time. So when people ask you a question like that, you need to breathe in and out several times. After having breathed in and out several times, I told the young people, "The Buddha told us that things are impermanent. The war is also impermanent. It has to end some time."

But the problem is: are we doing anything to help end the war? If we allow ourselves to be overwhelmed by the feeling of despair or anger, we can't help. We can even fuel the war and make it intensify or last longer. So the question is whether we can do something for peace, whether we can *be* something for peace.

When you produce a thought of compassion, of loving kindness, of understanding, that is peace. When you do something to help the victims of war, the children and adults, to suffer less, and when you bring food for refugee children, these are the kinds of action that can help relieve a situation of suffering. So in a difficult situation, it's crucial for you to find a way to practice peace. Even if you can only do it in a very restricted manner, it will help you survive. It will help you nourish hope. So I think it's very important not to allow ourselves to be carried away by the feeling of despair. We should learn how to bring peace into our bodies and our minds, so we're able to give rise to thoughts of compassion, words of compassion, and acts of compassion in our daily lives. That will inspire many people, and it will help them not to be drowned in the ocean of despair. Our thinking and acting show that the First Mindfulness Training is possible. If we have some peace within ourselves, in our way of thinking, speaking, and acting, we'll be able to influence people and inspire them to go in the same direction. Little by little, we can improve the situation.

GENEROSITY AND THE SECOND MINDFULNESS TRAINING

The second mindfulness training is about generosity, not stealing, not harming the environment, not being greedy, and the ability to be happy with a minimum of conditions. This is very important. With the second mindfulness training, we have to think of true happiness. When people practice wrong diligence it's because they have too much desire. And having too much desire, you don't have time to live your life, to love, and to experience, healing and transformation. You burn yourself with the fire of desire. This should be a bell of mindfulness for business leaders who work too hard. There are many such people in our world. They may be powerful. They may be very successful in their enterprises. But they suffer; they don't really live their lives. They don't have the time to practice the four aspects of true diligence, because they are caught in wrong diligence and they are consumed by their work.

Don't think that if you're poor you're helpless. I know of many rich and powerful people who suffer very deeply from loneliness, and many of them have committed suicide. They suffer, and they deserve our compassion. But in order to have compassion to offer to others, we have to offer it to ourselves first. We cultivate compassion by looking deeply to understand the suffering inside us and around us. You don't have to be rich to help people. In fact if you're too wealthy you can't help people. People who are rich want to continue being rich, so they invest all their time and energy in maintaining their wealth; they don't even have time to take care of themselves and their families, so how can they help other people? Being wealthy is not a good condition for spiritual life. To live simply and to be happy is something that is possible. When you transform yourself into a bodhisattva, you have a lot of power—not the power associated with fame and money, but the power that helps you be free and enables you to help and bring relief to many people.

LOVE AND THE THIRD MINDFULNESS TRAINING

If we really love others, we will try to protect ourselves and protect others from sexual misconduct. Sexual misconduct usually comes from violence, fear, and anger. It is not about sex or love. If true love and understanding are there, anger and violence decrease, and we do not act out of fear.

We have many kinds of energies in us, including the energies of anger, violence, and craving. But compassion is also a very strong energy. If you allow the energy of compassion to take over, you can spend all your twenty-four hours a day doing things that will benefit people.

We all have sexual energy. The ways we eat, play, and spend our time are big factors in how we handle our sexual energy. The way we serve, the way we spend our leisure time, and the way we pass our time when we're with others has a lot to do with it. This is an art. We shouldn't suppress any kind of energy in us, including sexual energy. But we're trying to be intelligent in the way we handle this energy. There are good kinds of energy, and there are energies that can disturb us. Mindfulness, concentration, and the time we spend together with other practitioners can help us tremendously. We should smile to our own energies and know that we have the capacity to handle them. "My dear energy, I know you are there. I am here for you. I will learn how to help and to take care of you. Together we can be in peace. And you can help me also. You are energy, and it's possible to transform one energy into another, like the wind can be transformed into electricity." So sexual energy can be transformed into the energy of compassion and acts of compassion. We only have to learn how to transform it. With a community, a Sangha, it's possible to learn. The way we eat, drink, and manage our leisure time; the way we work together; and the way we serve, will determine our success.

TRANSFORMING SUFFERING AND ABUSE

If you have experienced sexual abuse, the best way for you to get rid of your pain is to become a bodhisattva. You make a vow to protect individuals, couples, families, and children from sexual abuse. You try your best to protect people. When the energy of a bodhisattva is in you, the suffering of being a victim of sexual abuse will begin to dissolve.

There was a U.S. soldier whose whole platoon was killed during the Vietnam War. He blamed the villagers, and in revenge he put explosives in sandwiches and left them at the entrance to the village for the villagers to find and eat. But it was the village children who discovered the sandwiches and ate them. Soon they were screaming, moaning, holding their stomachs, and writhing on the ground. The parents came running to help. But the soldier knew there was nothing that could save the children. For decades after the war he was unable to tolerate being in the same room with children. If a child entered the room he was in, he would have to run out. He came to Plum Village to attend a Veterans' Retreat. It took many days before he was willing to tell his story. I said to him, "Yes, you have killed five children. But there are many children who are suffering and dying in this very moment, because they lack nutrition or medicine. You could save countless numbers of children right now." He made a deep vow to work to save children, and from that moment his guilt complex and his suffering began to dissolve.

As a victim of sexual abuse, you don't have to bear the suffering of your abuse forever. If you make the strong vow to be a bodhisattva, you find ways to protect children and others by any means possible. The energy of your vow will dissolve the suffering in you, and you will be free. Vow and aspiration are very important. They give you a lot of energy that is healing and transformative.

THE POWER OF COMMUNICATION AND THE FOURTH MINDFULNESS TRAINING

During Plum Village retreats for Palestinians and Israelis, the two groups are initially suspicious of each other and have trouble looking at each other. Both groups have suffered a lot, and each group believes that their suffering was caused by the other. We give each side plenty of time apart from each other to practice and a lot of support in using the practices of deep listening and loving speech.

When the two groups finally come together as one group to share their pain and suffering, one side uses loving speech, and one side uses compassionate listening, without interrupting. The outcome is wonderful. While listening, you recognize that those on the other side have suffered almost exactly the same way as you have. Before that, you may have thought that only your side suffered in that way. But now you see the other side has suffered exactly the same things—fear, anger, suspicion, and pain. So you begin to see them as human beings like you. When you begin to see them as human beings who also suffer, the intention to punish is no longer there, and you begin to look at them with the eyes of compassion. You may even be motivated by the desire to help relieve their suffering. That is the transformation you experience during the time you practice compassionate listening.

When you look at them now, you suffer much less, because you've been able to see the suffering in them and you see them as human beings like you. When they see your eyes, they feel that you are looking at them with love and not with suspicion, fear, or anger anymore. So transformation takes place on both sides. You will also have a chance to speak out, maybe next week. And you will tell them about your suffering, and they will listen. This practice of compassionate listening and loving speech is very important to liberate us from our fear, anger, and hatred. It has the power to restore communication.

In the beginning we may notice that others have many wrong perceptions. It's because they have suffered so much. That's why in their way of speaking there's still some bitterness and accusation. But because we're practicing mindfulness of compassion, we don't interrupt them, and we allow them to speak out so they suffer less. The outcome is that we recognize them as living beings who have a lot of suffering. We no longer have the intention to punish them. We have the intention to help. It's not our intention to make them suffer. On our side there is also fear and suspicion that makes us difficult for them. If we have a difficult relationship with our partner, or with our parents and family members, or even with someone from a group we think has hurt us and our family, it's always possible to restore communication and to reconcile by practicing compassionate listening and loving speech.

THE ETHICAL AND SPIRITUAL ASPECTS OF THE FIFTH MINDFULNESS TRAINING

Suppose you practice the fifth training and you've stopped drinking alcohol or using drugs. But you're suffering because you still have the desire to drink alcohol or use drugs. You're following the guideline, the precept, but you don't really see the value of it. You don't see that it's come from insight and it has a spiritual dimension. You refrain, because you know that it's good for your health to do so, but you suffer. However, if you understand the deep meaning of the training and the benefits it will bring you, you will be happy to stop taking in toxins.

It's like being a vegetarian. When you experience how wonderful it makes you feel to not harm animals or the environment, you're happy to eat vegetarian food. You don't suffer because you're not eating meat. Instead, you feel lucky to be able to eat in such a way that you don't cause suffering to other living beings. There is joy; there is insight; and there is compassion and spirituality in your eating. Eating becomes a very spiritual thing.

There is no barrier dividing the ethical and the spiritual—they are one. This is the reason we focus on happiness and well-being as the key to a global ethic. We practice the Five Mindfulness Trainings because we see that they increase our well-being. The insight of the Four Noble Truths eases our suffering. And there is no distinction between our own suffering and the suffering of the world. We act ethically because we're motivated by the insight we have into interbeing and nondiscrimination. Our insight causes our thoughts, speech, and physical actions to manifest in a way that brings wellbeing to the world and to ourselves. We act this way not because we think we have to or are told to, but as a result of our own insight. Our actions only bring about more wellbeing to ourselves and to the world.

8

SANGHA IS THE KEY

BUILDING OUR GLOBAL COMMUNITY

It is difficult to make change alone. In the Sangha—the community of people who share the path of spiritual practice—there is a powerful collective energy of mindfulness and concentration. It can help us make a breakthrough; it ignites our insight. We want to offer the path of the Buddha to the world. We want to use the kind of nonsectarian language by which we can share the wisdom of the Buddha with the world. Our practice together of walking, sitting, breathing, eating, or even brushing our teeth is very important. Our collective practice is the foundation of our success.

We can help each other not to sink into the past, and not to cling to our pain and sorrows of the past. Our community can be our refuge. When we practice with the Sangha, it's easier than practicing alone. The collective energy of the Sangha helps us to transform more quickly. Sometimes something may carry us away. But thanks to the collective practice, we can regain our solidity. Even if we're distracted, our Sangha can help us remember to come back to the present moment, to touch what is positive, to touch our own peace, and to see how to undo the difficulty.

THE BELOVED COMMUNITY

The Sangha doesn't need to be Buddhist. Buddhism is made of non-Buddhist elements anyway. When I met Martin Luther King, Jr., in Chicago in 1966, we spoke about Sangha building. We met and had tea together before going to a press conference. In that press conference, Martin Luther King came out against the Vietnam War. I told the press that his activities for civil rights and human rights went along perfectly with our efforts in Vietnam to stop the killing and bring peace to the land, and that we should support each other.

Martin Luther King, Jr., was young at the time, and I was also young. We spoke a few times about the beloved community. Without the beloved community nothing can be done. The beloved community is the Sangha. The Buddha couldn't have done anything without his Sangha. That's why, after his enlightenment, he went to the Deer Park near Benares, hoping to find his five former co-practitioners there, and he built a Sangha of six people in the Deer Park. The Sangha grew into a Sangha of 60 people, then 900, and in just one year there were 1,250 ordained members.

My last meeting with Martin Luther King, Jr., was in Geneva, just a few months before his assassination. We were both there to participate in a peace conference called Pacem in Terris, peace on earth. He invited me to come up to his room on the eleventh floor for breakfast. I was late because I'd been detained by journalists. When I finally came up to his room, he was still waiting, and he had kept my breakfast warm. When he was shot, I was in New York City, sick with the flu. I was in despair when I heard what had happened.

Now as I look back, I see that the seeds we planted have

not been lost. They have begun to sprout and grow. The beloved community, the expression he used for the Sangha, is there. You can recognize it as a Sangha, although it doesn't have that name.

Imagine the president of the United States being surrounded by many advisors, including advisors from industry and the military. He's a politician. Is the Sangha strong enough and present enough to help and support him so that he can remain himself? This is a question I have put to myself. We should do something to show him and our other political leaders that the Sangha is there, supporting them.

When the Buddha met King Prasenajit for the last time, it was in northern Koshala. During that meeting the king told the Buddha, "Lord Buddha, every time I see your Sangha I have more and more confidence in you." The Sangha was the work of the Buddha, and without the Sangha the Buddha would not have been able to realize his dream. Like Martin Luther King, Jr., the Buddha dreamed of relieving the world of suffering. It's a noble dream. Each of us can do something to help relieve the suffering in the world, but none of us can do it alone.

PRACTICING WITH THE SANGHA

In the Sangha there are those who bring happiness to many people. There are those monastics and laypeople who cook very well, and there are those who make wonderful bread. There are those who take care of the garden beautifully and grow wholesome nutritious organic vegetables. There are those who organize festivities in a very beautiful, creative way. There are those who don't have these talents, but when they do sitting meditation they are very happy, and when they walk they are also happy and this brings happiness to others. Such people are of great benefit to the Sangha.

Everybody contributes their part. You don't need to be exactly like others. This is true whether you are thinking of your family as your Sangha or of the larger beloved community. Everyone has their own abilities. Somebody must be the Sangha eyes; somebody must be the ears; somebody must be the feet; and somebody must be the hands. You don't need to be like others; you just need to be yourself. You contribute your own part as yourself. You don't need to have perfect health or a perfect mind without any worries and anxiety. You can still have some pain in your body or some pain in your mind. But thanks to the practice, you can create more joy, peace, and understanding that nourishes you, nourishes the Sangha, and nourishes the world.

THE HILL OF THE TWENTY-FIRST CENTURY

The twenty-first century is like a hill. And we are climbing the hill of the twenty-first century as a Sangha. I'm sure that if we continue to climb beautifully, enjoying every step, when we arrive and look down, it will be very beautiful. Everything depends on *how* we climb the hill of the century. Each step should be love. Each step should be forgiveness. Each step should be healing and transformation. We walk in such a way that each step brings peace, happiness, and awareness of our common humanity. We don't want to walk in any other way. We want to walk in such a way that every step becomes healing, nourishing, and transformative.

Every time we sit, we sit in such a way that the world can profit from our sitting. We are solid, relaxed, calm, and happy while sitting. We sit as though we are sitting on a lotus flower, and not on a heap of burning charcoal. When we eat our breakfast, we eat in such a way that makes peace, joy, and freedom possible—and that makes life possible, because when we're truly present we can enjoy all the wonders of life inside us and around us.

Eating our breakfast is a deep practice. You are always there for yourself and for your family, your community. You are not carried away by the past or by the future. You are really *there* in order to eat your breakfast. Your breakfast is available to you, and you are available to the breakfast. You are available to the Sangha, and the Sangha is there and available to you, always dwelling in the present moment. The Buddha said that the past is already gone and the future is not yet here, so there is only one moment when you can be truly alive, and that is the present moment. Therefore, our determination and practice are to always stay in the present moment. The present moment is the door to healing and transformation.

TOGETHER, WE MAKE THE WORLD

We hear of the suffering around the world and we want to help. The problem is that we are so busy. We have no time, no energy for our fellow human beings whether here or abroad. That is the main obstacle. Many of us feel we don't have enough time, even for ourselves and our family; so how can we reach out and help people across the world? How can we reach out to people who feel left alone in their struggles for democracy, independence, and so on? Our good intention is there. The willingness to help is there. But often we feel we don't have the means to help.

We need to liberate ourselves from our too-busy lives. We want to help others, but often we are so busy running around, we feel we don't have time to do anything else. As a Sangha, we can help each other prioritize healing the world. We can reorganize our individual and collective lives in order to be with each other in a more intimate and beneficial way.

Whether the twenty-first century becomes a century of spirituality depends on our capacity to build Sanghas. Without a Sangha, we will become victims of despair. We need each other. We need to congregate, to bring together our wisdom, our insight, and our compassion, and make the Sangha like a family. We should give up focusing only on our personal desires and see the Earth as our true home, a home for all of us. Now is the time when we have to build the Sangha of all nations. We invite everyone to look deeply into our situation. We invite everyone to speak out and spread the message. If we fail in this task of Sangha building, then the suffering of the twenty-first century will be indescribable.

ONE STEP

We must learn to speak out so that the voice of the Buddha, the voice of Jesus, the voice of Mohammad and all our spiritual ancestors can be heard in this dangerous and pivotal moment in history. We should offer our light to the world so it will not sink into total darkness. Everyone has the seed of awakening and insight within his or her heart. Let us help each other touch these seeds in ourselves and in others so that everyone will have the courage to speak out. We have the tools. We have the path. We have the ability—with practice—to have the insight. All we need to do is to begin. With one step, with one breath, we can commit to living our daily lives in a way that brings happiness and well-being to the planet, to our beloved communities, and to ourselves.

THE MANIFESTO 2000

Some years ago, I had the opportunity to sit down with many Nobel Peace Prize winners to discuss how to help transform violence in the world so that children will benefit. Together we drafted a text called the Manifesto 2000. We also proposed that the United Nations declare the first ten years of the twenty-first century to be a decade for nonviolence and peace. Our proposal was accepted by the United Nations, and they issued a decree, ARES 53129, declaring that the year 2000 be the International Year for the Culture of Peace, and that the decade 2001-2010 be the International Decade for the Promotion of the Culture of Nonviolence and Peace for the Children in the World.

Although we did not solve all the world's problems in these ten years, the Manifesto became a good guide that many people use. You may prefer using the language of the Manifesto 2000 to the Five Mindfulness Trainings, although the content is the same. So far seventy-five million people have signed the Manifesto, including heads of state and other prominent figures.

MANIFESTO 2000 FOR A CULTURE OF PEACE AND NONVIOLENCE

Because the year 2000 must be a new beginning, an opportunity to transform—all together—the culture of war and violence into a culture of peace and nonviolence;

Because this transformation demands the participation of each and every one of us, and must offer young people and future generations the values that can inspire them to shape a world based on justice, solidarity, liberty, dignity, harmony, and prosperity for all;

Because the culture of peace can underpin sustainable development, environmental protection, and the well-being of each person;

Because I am aware of my share of responsibility for the future of humanity, in particular to the children of today and tomorrow;

I pledge in my daily life, in my family, my work, my community, my country, and my region, to:

1) Respect the life and dignity of each human being without discrimination or prejudice.
2) Practice active nonviolence, rejecting violence in all its forms: physical, sexual, psychological, economic, and social, in particular towards the most deprived and vulnerable such as children and adolescents.
3) Share my time and material resources in a spirit of generosity to put an end to exclusion, injustice, and political and economic oppression.
4) Defend freedom of expression and cultural diversity, giving preference always to dialogue and listening without engaging in fanaticism, defamation, and the rejection of others.
5) Promote consumer behavior that is responsible and development practices that respect all forms of life and preserve the balance of nature on the planet.
6) Contribute to the development of my community, with the full participation of women and respect for democratic principles, in order to create together new forms of solidarity.

Dharmacharya Shantum Seth, a teacher ordained by Thich Nhat Hanh, offers teachings and shares the practice of Mindfulness meditation in different parts of India and the world. He also leads pilgrimages, 'In the Footsteps of the Buddha'.

Please visit: www.buddhapath.com or contact info@buddhapath.com

Ahimsa Trust represents Thich Nhat Hanh and his community in India. It is a volunteer driven, non-profit trust, working to create peace, in one's self and in the world. Ahimsa Trust organizes Days of Mindfulness and retreats/workshops across India, especially for educators.

Please visit www.ahimsatrust.org or contact ahimsa.trust@gmail.com

For worldwide contacts and teachings of Thich Nhat Hanh and his community, please visit www.plumvillage.org